Communication Skills

for the 21st Century

How to Understand and be Understood

by

Bill R. Swetmon

Skill-Speak Press
2520 Ave. K, Suite 702
Plano, Texas 75074

Library of Congress Cataloging-in-Publication Data

Swetmon, Bill.
   Communication skills for the 21st century : how to understand and be understood / by Bill R. Swetmon.
     p. cm.
   Includes bibliographical references and index.
   ISBN 0-9662070-0-9 (pbk. : alk. paper)
    1.   Interpersonal communication. 2. Business communication.
3. Success in business. I. Title.
BF637.C45s865   1998
302.2—dc21   97-51884
                                                                                   CIP

© 1998 Skill-Speak Press

All Rights Reserved

No part of this book may be reproduced in any form or by any means without permission in writing from Skill-Speak Press.

Printed in the United States of America

ISBN 0-9662070-0-9
10 9 8 7 6 5 4 3 2 1
9712

All inquiries for volume purchases of this book should be addressed to:
Skill-Speak, Inc.
2520 Ave. K, Suite 702
Plano, Texas 75074

Cover photo by Roger Goldingay
© 1994 Aris Multimedia Entertainment, Inc.

Table of Contents

About The Author vi
Introduction vii
Chapter 1—How to Communicate with Powerful Public Speaking................................... 1
   Dealing With Anxiety 2
      The Method 3
      The Greek Factor.............................. 5
      Open With a Power Punch 6
      Remember The Rule Of Three 6
      Make it Visual 7
      The Importance of The Voice 8
      Close With a Sinker.......................... 11
      Audience Motivation 13
      Why Audiences Don't Listen................... 14
      You Can't Fool the Audience 16
      The Joy of Speaking 17
Chapter 2—How to Communicate with Your Body 19
   The Vocabulary of Positive Body Language.............. 20
   The Vocabulary of Negative Body Language 22
   International Gestures 23
   Speaking with Handshakes 25
   Working a Room................................... 27
Chapter 3—How to Communicate with an Appealing Personality 31
   Assertiveness/Passiveness/Aggressiveness.............. 31
   Assertive Characteristics 32
   Assertiveness in Confrontation...................... 34
   Assertiveness Begins with Equality.................. 38
   Positive Self-Talk.................................. 39
   How to Begin 40
   Anger and Assertiveness........................... 42

Chapter 4—How to Communicate with a Professional Writing Style **45**
    The First Alphabet 45
    Modern Writing 45
    The Most Important Key........................ 46
    Let Your Writing Flow 47
    Top-Down Writing 48
    Active Voice 49
    Eliminate Wordiness—Prune and Sharpen.......... 51
    Gender-Free Writing............................ 56
    Give the Reader Air............................ 57
    Go the Extra Mile 58

Chapter 5—How to Communicate with Proper Grammar... **61**
    The Basics 62
    Where it All Begins 65
    Punctuating Sentences 67
    The Comma 68
    The Semicolon 70
    The Colon 70
    The Ellipsis 72
    The Hyphen 72
    The Parentheses 73
    The Dash 74
    The Brackets 74
    The Quotation Marks 74
    The Question Mark 75
    The Exclamation Mark 76
    The Apostrophe 76
    Common Errors 77
    Capitalization 80

Chapter 6—How to Communicate with Proper Etiquette.. **83**
    Table and Eating Manners 84

    Proper Introductions 88
    Global Respect 88
    Diversity in the Workplace 90
    Job Interview 91
    Travel 94
    Little Things Count 96

Chapter 7—How to Communicate with
Effective Leadership **97**
    Emotional Intelligence 99
    People Skills 103

Chapter 8—How to Communicate with
Outstanding Customer Service **113**
    Customer Service: A Definition 114
    The Dissatisfied Customer 116
    The Customer is Always Right 120
    Begin a Customer-Obsessed MovemenT 121
    Hiring Customer-Loving People 123
    Creating a Customer-Centered Culture 124
    Identifying Marks of Service Quality 127

Chapter 9—How to Communicate with Good
Health and Nutrition **129**
    Exercise 129
    Nutrition 133
    Stress 140

Chapter 10—How to Communicate with
Strong Emotion **143**
    Happiness is a Choice 150
    Traits of Happy People 150
    The Spiritual Life 153

Appendix —How to Communicate as an
Emphatic Listener **159**
Bibliography **163**
Index **165**

Dedication

This book is dedicated to you, the reader, who obviously cares about your relationship with others. May you enjoy the thrill of learning more about the incredibly challenging and rewarding field of human communications.

About the Author

Bill Swetmon has prepared the material for this book from a wide spectrum of careers: television producer/director; author of six other books; commercial talent for broadcast and print; corporate trainer; motivational speaker; and management consultant. He is the President and CEO of Skill-Speak, Inc., a company dedicated to excellence in communication and public speaking through seminars, training, and communication resources. Bill holds a bachelor of arts in communication and a master of science in counseling psychology. He is a member of the World Future Society and a professional member of the National Speakers Association. He travels nationally and internationally for his speaking engagements.

His topics cover a wide area of interest:
- How to Speak with Confidence and Power
- Personality Plus Communication Equals Success
- Business Etiquette for the Busy Person
- How to Give Excellent Customer Service
- Management and Leadership Principles for the New Millennium
- Training Techniques to Become a Better Trainer
- How to Be a Better Communicator
- Overcoming Communication Problems
- Business Writing Made Easy
- Managing Conflict in the Workplace
- How to Stay Young Through Proper Health and Nutrition
- How to Become an Emphatic Listener
- How to Supervise People and Get Results!

Introduction

Communication Skills for the 21st Century is a "working with people" book designed to do just that, help you, the reader, to work more effectively and efficiently with others. Here are some things you'll learn:

- What characterizes a confident person?
- What are the do's and don'ts of a successful job interview?
- How do you give a powerful speech with confidence and without anxiety?
- How do you know if the person you're speaking to is listening?
- What is proper etiquette at a business luncheon and a formal meal?
- How do you confidently express your ideas?
- What can you say to calm an irate customer?
- How can you control your emotions and not allow the emotions of others to control you?
- How do you use a pause in conversation to process information?
- How can you know for sure what the other person is trying to say?
- How do you correctly read body language? For example, what do the arms folded across the chest *really* mean?
- What are the qualities of futuristic leaders?
- How can you keep your body young and healthy?
- How do you communicate your ideas in writing so others will want to read what you've written?
- Are there sure ways to write grammatically correct sentences without memorizing an entire textbook?
- How do you overcome the #1 marital problem today?

Communication Skills for the 21st Century

This is the only book available today dealing with every aspect of human communication. You'll immediately enhance all your communication skills, and you'll use it over and over as a reference—so keep it in your desk, briefcase, purse, or on the bedside table. Refer to it often—discover the joy and success of an effective communicator!

Bill R. Swetmon, 1998

Chapter 1

How to Communicate with Powerful Public Speaking

The ability to speak before a group is the most sought after skill in the business world today, and so few are able to do it well. Daniel Webster once observed, "If all my talents and powers were to be taken from me by some unscrupulous Providence, and I had my choice of keeping but one, I would unhesitatingly ask to be allowed to keep the power of speaking, for through it, I would quickly recover all the rest." Webster obviously realized the importance of good communication skill, and how with it one can develop many other talents and powers.

The ability to stand before a group of people and express one's ideas in such a way as to motivate the listeners to respond positively to what is being said is a valuable asset. Think back over your own life and the many different speakers you've heard through school and into your adult years. Perhaps you have heard 400 or more speakers counting all your teachers, the politicians running for office, preachers, lecturers, etc. How many of them were able to do it well enough you can remember them today? You can probably count the number on one hand.

In today's world very few make it to the top without first making it to their feet! Because of the need for excellence in public speaking, this chapter will focus on the skills one needs in order to do this wonderful work well and effectively. The skills set forth here can assist one in reaching many goals and aspirations in life. Study this chapter carefully and apply these techniques at every opportunity. You will discover an exciting transformation taking place in your ability to move and motivate an audience.

Dealing With Anxiety

The research is in and the verdict is: Everyone suffers with *Laliophobia*—the fear of public speaking! There is no exception. As a matter of fact, it is the number one fear—winning out over such things as heights, insects, bugs, financial problems, deep water, sickness, and death. We are more afraid of speaking before a group than of dying; perhaps because we may have to speak publicly many times and die only once!

In any case, there is a great fear of public speaking.

This fear has been called the "Fight or Flight Syndrome." When the human body is in a state of fear and anxiety, several physiological responses begin to take place all at once. The brain's cortex sends a signal to the sympathetic nervous system to be on alert and prepare for action. The adrenal glands begin to pump out stress hormones which trigger a chain reaction. The heart rate increases; the blood pressure rises; the adrenaline increases in the bloodstream; the blood begins to recirculate, filling the nerve endings in the stomach, better know as butterflies.

The first step in calming down all these activities and becoming more relaxed is to give this event a different name. Instead of calling it fear or nervousness, let's call it POWER!

The name you give to something or someone determines how you view that object or person. A positive name produces a positive reaction; a negative name produces a negative reaction.

So from now on call nervousness POWER.

This power gives you the ability to overcome the number one fear: the audience. Why are we so afraid of the audience? We fear...

- They will not like us.
- They will think we are foolish or at least not very intelligent.
- They will laugh at our mistakes.
- They will know we have forgotten our train of thought.
- They will be bored with our material.

- They will decide if we are a good speaker or a bad speaker and react accordingly.
- They will know we are nervous.

All of these fears are called: the Voice of Judgment. It is that voice inside us that judges us harshly and believes everyone else judges us the same way, which is not true. Most audiences don't judge speakers as severely as the speaker judges himself or herself. As a matter of fact, most audiences are neutral. If the speaker does a few things right at the very beginning, the audience will be in total support, regardless of what happens during the rest of the presentation.

So the first thing you must learn to do is control your attitude toward the audience by using your nervousness as a powerful and energetic source of strength in order to do a great job communicating to your audiences.

The Method

It all begins with your attitude toward the audience.

Every great Hollywood actor is familiar with the Method. This is a form of acting that utilizes "sense memory." Developed by a Russian director named Konstantin Stanislavsky, the Method is a way for the actor to identify with the character in the play or movie by thinking in terms of "as if." The actor strives to act "as if" he or she is feeling the same emotion the character in the play or movie is feeling. The actor develops his/her sense memory or emotional memory, which is the ability to go back in one's life and think about an experience in which the same emotion was felt. The actor dwells on that experience until the emotion becomes so real the actor is actually reliving it all over again. Bruce Dern, a Method-trained actor, feels that the Method gives the actor a spontaneity that adds to the performance.

The basis for developing a character through Method acting is for the actor to use his/her own characteristics, personality, style, and emotions. For instance, an actor playing Hamlet feels his own vacillation that identifies with Hamlet's vacillation, his own ambition that permeates the character of Hamlet. The actor adds his or her own colors to the tapestry of the character, which gives the character a realistic depth that would not normally be there.

The actor then brings that emotion into the scene in which the character being played by the actor is going through a similar feeling. When the audience watches the actor, they sense the realism of the scene because the actor is actually *feeling* the emotion of the moment.

The power of this form of acting was demonstrated in the great actress Meryl Streep on the set of *Ironwood*, a bleak film in which she played a ragged outcast during the Depression who dies in a cheap hotel room. According to an article in *Life* magazine, Ms. Streep hugged a giant bag of ice cubes to simulate the feeling of lifelessness. In the dramatic scene, her hobo husband, played by Jack Nicholson, cried and sobbed, shaking her lifeless body. When the scene was finished, Ms. Streep just lay on the bed cold and still. After about ten minutes, she began to emerge from a deep, trance-like state which she had entered emotionally and psychologically.

According to Brad Darrach, author of the *Life* article, Meryl Streep looks, speaks, thinks, moves, and feels like the characters she plays. She is endowed with magnificent powers of self-transformation. Sydney Pollack, the Oscar-winning director, says that Meryl Streep can actually vanish into another person.

A public speaker can also connect to his/her audience by using a similar power to present material so it will be believed and experienced by the audience. In order for that to happen, some important attitudes must be developed by the speaker toward the audience. Here are the keys ones:

- The audience is on my side, not against me.
- The audience needs to hear what I am presenting.
- I care for the audience.
- I am glad to be able to present this material.
- I have prepared my material and it is good stuff!
- I feel good about who I am and how I appear.

- I can *see* myself doing a good job.
- I am excited and passionate about my presentation.
- I am committed to doing my very best. The audience *will* like me!

If a speaker can check off all nine of these items each time before getting up to speak, the audience will be delighted with the presentation. If any one of these items is missing or cannot be affirmed, the presentation is in trouble before the speech begins!

Then, in addition to these, the speaker should recall a past experience of successful performance. It does not necessarily have to be public speaking. In recalling that experience, the speaker should try to remember the feelings of joy, pride, and confidence which that successful effort produced. Those feelings of success and positive self-esteem can be tapped into so the same feelings can be brought into the present to provide a confidence factor that would otherwise not be there.

The Greek Factor

The Greeks were great orators. They described effective public speaking with three words: ethos, pathos, and logos. Ethos refers to the things the speaker believes and is willing to present with courage. Pathos refers to the strong feelings the speaker has for the topic; a willingness to put one's heart into it. Logos refers to the words the speaker uses to formulate the thoughts; in other words, the speaker uses the brain to form the ideas.

Courage—heart—a brain. Sound familiar? Sure it does... *The Wizard of Oz!*

Here are the sources every speaker can use to turn nervousness into power. When a speaker realizes that every person in the audience has some goals—in other words, is on the Yellow Brick Road of life, and that speaker endeavors to connect to those goals through ethos, pathos, and logos (courage, heart, brain), the presentation will be powerful because it will meet people where they live! They will sense the speaker cares for them and is interested in their lives and knows things that will help them reach their goals. Who would not want to listen to such a person?

In order to make the presentation appealing and interesting, there are some important tips to keep in mind.

Open With A Power Punch

The most listened to sentence in the entire speech is the first one! It is also the one most speakers waste with weak, boring words such as: *Good morning, how are you today? It is good to be with you, etc., etc., etc.*

Dynamic speakers have learned the importance of opening with a power punch, the kind Mike Tyson would use in his first round of boxing that usually resulted in the opponent looking at the stars! A power punch is simply an opening statement that grabs attention, creates interest, and hooks the audience as they are trying to decide whether to listen attentively to the rest of the speech.

The importance of this opening sentence cannot be overstated. Whether it is a quote, a story, an illustration, or a funny line, the audience will decide from it whether the remainder of the speech is important. If the opening statement is done well, the speaker has bought a few minutes of time to prove to the audience that it will be worth their time to listen to the rest of the presentation. Therefore, much effort and energy should be spent in preparing and memorizing that opening sentence.

Remember The Rule Of Three

The rule of three is a little known fact: The average person has to hear something at least three times in order to remember it. Some people can remember things after hearing them once, a few can remember better after a second time; most people must hear things at least three times in order to remember the information.

Public speakers who remember the rule of three will tell the audience at the very beginning what they are going to hear. Then, during the body of the presentation, the material will be presented a second time, and then at the close the speaker will wrap up with a third reminder of the material. When the audience hears it for the third time, they will remember. Every good speaker keeps the rule of three in mind as the presentation is being developed and presented.

Some speakers like to keep the material concealed and reveal it as they move through the presentation, as though there is some value and excitement in the anticipation. To some extent, this is true. And perhaps there are some strictly entertaining speeches that fit into this type of delivery. But most speeches are delivered for people to remember. In order for most people to remember, they must hear the information at least three times.

So as the old cliché goes: Tell them what you are going to tell them; then tell them; then tell them what you've told them. When you do this, they will remember it.

Make It Visual

People take in information through three sensors: auditory (listening); visual (seeing); kinesthetic (feeling and doing). A good communicator will remember all three of these while preparing and delivering the material.

The auditory refers to the words. A good vocabulary and command of the English language are vitally important. Choosing the right words for the right ideas separates good speakers from mediocre speakers. Expressing those words in sentences with proper grammar and usage polishes off the speech in a professional manner. There are other sections of this book that will deal with these areas, so time will not be spent on them here. It should be emphasized when a speaker uses poor grammar and limited vocabulary, it reflects on the individual and detracts from the presentation.

In addition to the words the speaker chooses, the visual and kinesthetic add spice and appeal to the speech. We live in a visual age. People are accustomed to *seeing* as well as *hearing*. It has been said a picture is worth a thousand words, and in some cases that is true. Some people remember better what they see than what they hear. And if there is emotion involved, the memory is enhanced even more.

Adding visuals to one's presentation will almost guarantee a better retention of the material by the average audience. Visual aids come in many different forms:

- Transparencies
- PowerPoint (computer generated visuals)
- Flip charts
- Slides
- Video
- Handouts (outlines, in-depth materials, etc.)
- Film
- Show 'n Tell (any illustration the audience can see).

But the most important visual is YOU the presenter!

Research has shown that people form opinions based on the following impressions: 7 percent from what is said, 38 percent from impressions received from the sound of the voice, and 55 percent from what they see. So 93 percent of the impressions formed about the message and the messenger is formed by nonverbals (vocal and visual). Only 7 percent is from the verbal! But without the verbal, there is no message; so even though it is a small percentage of the total message, the verbal carries tremendous importance. After the message has been well prepared, the key to its overall success is the *packaging*.

The Importance Of The Voice

If the speaker presents the material with an exciting, warm, friendly voice, and if the body language is open and positive (i.e., smiles often, has a pleasant demeanor, uses limited and meaningful gestures with open posture), the audience will feel positive about the presentation.

The voice is a very important part of a good speech. This does not mean one must have a beautiful, golden voice in order to communicate effectively. A good voice can be developed through a few simply techniques.

Breathing

In order to breathe properly, the breath should be drawn deeply into the lungs (called deep-body breathing). To determine if you are breathing properly, place one hand on your upper chest and the other hand on your stomach. Down breathe deeply. If the chest rises, you are breathing improperly. To breathe properly, draw the air deep down into the lower part off the body; therefore, the stomach should push out and the chest should remain the same—not rise and fall as you breathe. By practicing deep-body breathing, the voice takes on a richer quality and you are able to use the air efficiently as it is pushed up through the throat into the mouth, nasal passages, past the teeth, tongue, and out through the lips and nose. You will also be able to raise and lower the voice for proper effect without shouting or speaking too low.

Open Oral Resonance

In order to make the voice sound interesting, it should resonate throughout the entire upper body and face, not just the throat. In order for that to happen, you must open your mouth wider than normal and form your words from the back of the throat all the way to the front of the mouth. There are several areas involved in this process:

1. Inhalation (breathing in); 2. Exhalation (breathing out); 3. Phonation (pushing the air from the lungs past the two vocal cords); 4. Resonation (the sound waves amplified in the cavities of throat, mouth, and nose); 5. Articulation (forming the words with the lips, jaws, teeth, and plates). Open oral resonance involves opening the mouth, separating the teeth, raising the tongue in front, and lowering the tongue in the back as you form your words.

Intonation

Intonation means the raising and lowering and the altering of the voice tone. This is especially important because nothing is more boring than a speaker who talks in a monotone. Intonation adds meaning to the message by putting emphasis on certain words or phrases. This is not done by shouting at the audience. Many audiences find shouting offensive. If you want to get your audience to listen to a particular point and remember it, lower your voice slightly and speak slowly and deliberately. An audience will remember a whisper longer than a shout! Intonation matches the tone of the voice with the meaning you intend to give to a word or phrase.

Pauses

You've heard the old saw: Silence is golden. When it comes to powerful presentation skill, one of the most effective skills a speaker can develop is *pausibility*. When a speaker talks nonstop, the audience will soon feel overloaded. Pauses give the audience a rest, a breather. The fear of silence causes many speakers to use "killer fillers," sounds to fill in the empty spaces such as: "ers," "ums," and "ahs." The silent pause gives the audience a chance to catch up with you and think about what you've just said. It also gives you a breather so you can think of the next point, relax a bit, and breathe. It also helps tremendously if you have lost your train of thought. You can preface the pause with a brief review of what you've just said, and then introduce the next point with a question or an introductory statement: "We have looked at three ways to deal with this problem. Now let's look at still another way... (pause—gather your thoughts)."

Rate of Speech/Volume

The rate you speak is important. If you are too slow, the audience has too much time to wander away; if you speak too rapidly, some have a hard time concentrating. If you speak too loudly, it irritates some people; if you speak too softly, some will not be able to hear. So it is important to vary the rate of speech as well as the volume. Practice makes perfect. Rehearsing your material with audio and video recordings will help you discover the proper rate and volume that are just right for you.

The voice can also be used to create a very important visual—the Theater of the Mind. Good speakers have learned the art of movie production: forming mental images on the screen of the brain for the audience to see and feel. Some of those images can be formed through:

- Personal stories and illustrations that touch the heart/emotion of the audience
- Quotes from famous people
- Anecdotes
- Humor that enlightens through laughter
- Drawing meaningful images through creative choice of words/phrases

These visuals will ensure the message stays with the audience long after the presentation is over. Remember that 6-8 minutes are about as long as any audience can concentrate without something interesting grabbing their attention. Every 6-8 minutes you should insert a story, an illustration, a visual, a joke, or even a change in the rate of speech and a lowering or raising of the voice. These will bring their attention back to what you are saying.

Close With A Sinker

A good presentation contains a great "hook," an interesting "line" with visuals, and a powerful "sinker" that puts the message down where the people live. The most important part of a speech is the close. That is the part most remembered because it is the last thing heard. Sadly, many speakers pay very little if any attention to the close.

Some speakers don't know how to close, so they just stop talking and sit down. While most people are no doubt grateful the speaker finally stopped, the audience will remember very little of what was said if the close has been weak.

Stephen Covey, in his outstanding work *The 7 Habits of Highly Effective People,* stated that highly effective people always begin with the end in mind. They know where they are going before they start. The same could be said of highly effective speakers . . . they know where they are going from the very beginning. The close is the target.

All of us have heard speakers who did not know where they were going, so like the energized bunny—they kept going and going and going.

Albert Einstein was the original absentminded professor. He often forgot his apartment number while living on campus at Princeton University. He would call the switchboard operator to ask for the apartment number. She would remind him to write it down, and he would agree, but for some reason he never remembered to do so. One day, the story is told, Dr. Einstein was on a train, and the conductor came by for the ticket. Dr. Einstein had misplaced it from the time he purchased it to the time he got on the train. As he searched frantically for the ticket, the conductor recognized him and said, "Aren't you Dr. Albert Einstein?" "Yes, yes," Dr. Einstein replied. "And I seem to have lost my ticket." "That's okay," the conductor said. "I know you wouldn't be on this train if you hadn't bought a ticket. So it is okay, I don't need it." Later the conductor came back through the car, and now Dr. Einstein was going through all his books looking for the ticket. The conductor reminded him that it was not important, he didn't need the ticket. Dr. Einstein replied, "It is important! I need to know where I'm to get off this train!"

In a similar way, every speaker needs to know where to get off the train—and that is the purpose of the close.

But the close is more than the end, it is also a review—a reminder for retention. It tells the audience what they have just heard. It reinforces the information which has been presented in the main body of the talk. But even more than that, it is an assignment—telling the audience what they should do as a result of what they have heard. It is a call to action!

An effective close *must* include the following:

- A review of the main points of the message

- An application/assignment for the audience to apply to their personal lives
- An appropriate story/anecdote/quote to end presentation
- A genuine thank you

Henry Wadsworth Longfellow said, "Great is the art of b e g i n n i n g . . . but greater is the art of ending."

Audience Motivation

Tom Leech, in *How to Prepare, Stage, and Deliver Winning Presentations* (AMACON, 1982, p. 71), has given five levels of audience motivation.

1. Listen. Make sure your audience is listening to you. One way to know you have their attention is to look at each one individually (good eye contact!). If you catch them looking back at you, you can be fairly sure they are listening. Then you take them to the next level.
2. Understand. Remember the K.I.S.S. formula: keep it simple and sweet. It is important to communicate to your audience in such a way each person knows and comprehends what you are saying. Remember the reading level of the average person is eighth grade. That means the average sentence should be about 15-18 words in length, and each word should be about 1.5 syllables. The same formula should apply to public speakers. Keep your sentences fairly short and your words simple. That will lead you to the next level.
3. Believe. The audience will believe what you say if they can believe in you. By following the suggestions in this chapter, you should be able to deliver believable presentations. But the key to that depends on your personal character. Somehow an audience can determine the reliability of a speaker by a "sixth" sense.
4. Retain. If your presentation is delivered with the "rule of three," they will be able to retain what they heard. Be sure

to remind them of the key areas you want them to remember.
   5. Act or do. This is the final level. Be sure to give your audience something to do or to act on after they leave. The way you extend your presentation beyond the initial hearing of the message is to have an assignment for everyone. If nothing other than reviewing their notes, it would be worthwhile to ask them to do that.

Why Audiences Don't Listen

There are many reasons audiences don't listen. Ronald Alder and Neil Towne, in the textbook *Looking Out, Looking In* (Harcourt Brace Jovanovich, 1993), p. 253, gave some reasons why people don't listen well to speakers:

   1. Message overload. Someone has said the mind can only comprehend what the seat can endure—or something to that effect. The average person can give fairly good attention to a speaker for about 20 minutes. Beyond that, the speaker will have to be extremely interesting and exciting to keep their attention simply because they will feel overloaded. There is only so much information the brain can receive at any one time.
   2. Preoccupation. Every person sitting in your audience has a particular set of problems, challenges, and difficulties in life. As the audience listens to your presentation, there is a temptation to think about many other things that are bearing down on their minds, rather than what you may be saying at that moment.
   3. Rapid thinking. The average person can think at about 700-1000 words per minute and listen at about 400 words per minute. On an average, people speak at about 140 words per minute. So while you are speaking, the audience can be thinking ahead of you, or listening to you and thinking about many other things at the same time. Zig Ziglar uses unusual body movements to bring his listeners' attention back to his topic every 30 seconds or so. He

squats down low, then stands up, he moves around the stage. It's an interesting method. As one of the highest-paid sales speakers in the world, he is unquestionably effective.

4. Effort. It takes effort to listen to another person. When you are listening to a speaker for any length of time, your heart rate increases, your respiration sometimes will increase. It is difficult for most people to keep this going for a long time.

5. External noise. This can be any type of distracting sounds, either in the room or outside. But there are some that are speaker noises, such as fiddling with a pen, putting the eye-glasses on and pulling them off, rattling change in the pocket, or wearing brightly colored clothes.

6. Hearing problems. Fifty percent of people have hearing problems. This, of course, makes it difficult to understand the speaker's words. The attention span is shortened considerably when the person has to strain to hear.

7. Faulty assumptions. This is an assumption of what was said, which can be in error.

8. Lack of apparent advantage. The listener does not understand the benefits of what is being said. The speaker has failed to explain the value of the presentation to the listener; consequently, when value is not recognized or appreciated, there is very little attention given to what is being said.

9. Lack of training. Most people have had courses in school in reading, writing, arithmetic, spelling, etc. But I would venture to say you have never had a course on listening. Most people don't know how to listen to a speaker. Yet, statistics tells us that 32 percent of our time is spent listening, and 21 percent of our time is in face-to-face listening. That's a total of 53 percent of our time spent in doing something for which most have received no training. It is a challenge to reach an audience and keep their attention when they don't know how to listen to you!

Communication Skills for the 21st Century

Ron Hoff wrote a very interesting book on public speaking—*I Can See You Naked*. There is a section of the book called "Picking up a few tricks from the dogs of Oshkosh." Here is what Ron wrote:

"Maybe your next presentation should go to the dogs. When two dogs made their entrance at a business meeting I was attending recently, I jotted down a few things about their presentation technique:

1. Dogs always seem so glad to see you. (I've excused pit bulls from this analysis.)
2. There is no artifice or pretense about their greeting. They just come right up to you and make friends. They communicate friendly little noises—but never give you a long line of guff.
3. They show the same affectionate attention to everybody. They're demonstrative without being pushy.
4. Their message is simple: We like you. We like being here.
5. They have no hidden agendas.
6. Their body language is telegraphic.
7. They don't do most of the things that dull presenters do: they don't carry scripts, don't monotone endlessly about themselves, don't lean on podiums, don't tell bad jokes or endless stories (not even endless shaggy dog stories).
8. Dogs have a great sense of knowing when they're no longer the center of attraction. They just go over and lie down. They don't go overtime.
9. They know who they are. Most of them have endearing personalities.
10. They're good friends. They don't come in, put on a show, and hurry out to a waiting limo or taxicab. They'll stay with you as long as you need them."

You Can't Fool The Audience

There is an old saying that goes something like this: *You can fool some of the people all of the time, and all of the people some of the time, but you cannot fool all the people all the time!* The same thing can be said about audiences. There are certain things they know about the speaker without ever being told.

1. The audience knows your feelings. They watch your body language and facial expressions, listen to the sound of your voice, and sense your energy level. Within about 2 minutes they will decide what they think about you based on the "feelings" they receive from you. Then they will facially and physically feed those feelings back to you.
2. The audience knows how you feel about them. They pick up on subtle indicators of how you react to their questions, or how you respond to their statements (or in a thousand other ways), and decide you don't really care about their feelings or about them personally.
3. The audience knows when you are not being truthful. When you fail to make good eye contact, and your voice grows weak, these are sure signs to the audience that you are lying to them.
4. The audience knows when you lose interest in the presentation. I recently heard about a well-known speaker who became frustrated because his overhead projector slides were not available. He did not discover this until he was well into his speech. His anger was apparent in his voice and his frustration level was felt by the entire audience. As a result, he lost interest in what he was presenting and so did the audience. Some walked out on him!

The Joy Of Speaking

There is perhaps no more rewarding experience than standing before a group of people presenting your ideas and afterward, hearing and seeing the effect the presentation had on the audience. There are no words that describe the fulfillment and satisfaction such an experience can have on your self-esteem.

Someone has written:

Every speaker has a mouth,
An arrangement rather neat.
Sometimes it's filled with wisdom,
Sometimes it's filled with feet.

Every person reading these words has a great deal of wisdom to share with others. When it is done without opening the mouth and inserting a foot, the event can be a thrilling experience. Follow the guidelines in this chapter, and that goal will be reached without fear or failure!

Chapter 2

How to Communicate with Your Body

There are two languages that every person speaks: verbal and nonverbal. The non-verbal has been called: body language. Dr. Albert Mehrabian, former professor of Psychology at the University of California, Los Angeles, is known for his pioneering work in the field of nonverbal communication (body language). His experiments helped identify nonverbal and subtle ways in which one conveys like and dislike, power and leadership, discomfort and insecurity, social attractiveness, or persuasiveness.

Dr. Mehrabian found that the total impact of a message is about 7 percent verbal (words only) and about 38 percent vocal (including tone of voice, inflection and other sounds) and 55 percent nonverbal.

We talk (speak words) a total of about ten or eleven minutes a day, and an average sentence is only about 2.5 seconds. So the biggest part of our communication (the nonverbal) is what communicates our most powerful messages. You have probably heard many times that people remember more of what they see than what they hear. After a meeting we may forget the exact words someone used, but we retain for a long time the vivid image of that person's facial expressions.

Through life experiences we have learned, perhaps unconsciously, that people often lie with words (little white lies and omissions that are part of many conversations). But facial expressions and body language tend to be more honest. We believe a person when the words and body language are consistent; we doubt the person when the words and body language say different things.

As an example, picture this scene: You meet a co-worker in the office and ask how she did in the performance review. The friend says, "Okay." But her smile turns into a frown and her hand tightens around the book she is carrying. Did your friend really do "Okay" in the performance review? Probably not, but she does not want to talk about her true feelings, at least at that moment. When a person's facial expression and body language differ from the words, your experience tells you to go with the visual cues, not the words.

Dr. Alfred Adler has observed that posture (body language) shows how the person has trained the senses and how that person is using them to select impressions. Therefore, according to Adler, every posture, every facial expression has a meaning. Dr. Paul Ekman, of the University of California at San Francisco, has studied facial expressions extensively. He mapped out a technique for coding facial expressions called FACS, Facial Action Coding System, based on the role of the facial muscles in expressing different emotions. His research reveals seven emotions that are universal: sadness, happiness, anger, interest, fear, contempt, and surprise. Dr. Lillian Glass has added to this list love, doubt, compassion, boredom, and distracting interest. Each of these emotions is communicated nonverbally through body language and facial expressions.

Once you become acquainted with the basic types of body language, you are then able to study the way people communicate in different settings. Hidden and nonverbal messages are read clearly by watching the consistency of the body movements and the facial expressions. Dr.Adler's comment that every posture has a meaning is no doubt true, but one should be careful drawing quick conclusions simply by observing a particular movement or expression. By observing a person for a few minutes, you will be able to see a consistent series of patterns develop. Then conclusions can be drawn about what is going on inside the individual.

The Vocabulary of Positive Body Language

The following postures reflect a positive and confident attitude.

Smile: Nothing communicates more clearly than a smile. It communicates warmth, love, care, friendliness, positive self-esteem, etc. Professional singers discovered that a smile not only makes them look better, but it also improves the quality of their voices. You can actually *hear* a smile. You hear the smile when someone is talking on the telephone or the radio, because a voice coming through a smile sounds warm and friendly. A smile is also hard to fake; it is, in fact, easy to spot. You sense it subconsciously.

If you want to communicate a strong, positive presence, develop your smileability!

Open Posture: Allan Pease, in his book *Signals,* writes about research conducted into the folded-arms position. A group of students was asked to attend a series of lectures, and each student was instructed to keep the legs uncrossed, arms unfolded, and to take a casual, relaxed sitting position. At the end of the lectures each student was tested on retention, knowledge of the subject matter, and the attitude toward the lecturer. A second group of students was put through the same process, but these students were instructed to keep their arms tightly folded across their chests throughout the lectures. The results showed that the group with the folded arms had learned and retained 38 percent less than the group who kept its arms unfolded. The second group also had a more critical opinion of the lectures and of the lecturers. This research demonstrates what we've known for some time: Closing the body off by folding the arms reflects more negative thoughts. The very act of crossing the arms in front of the body may enhance and confirm the negative, withdrawn feelings inside. Many people have found this to be a very comfortable position in which to stand or sit, but that's because it is comfortable to have the body correspond with the feelings inside.

Eye Contact: Looking the person in the eyes, particularly when the person is talking, communicates interest in what the person is saying. But proper eye contact also involves looking away occasionally, especially when you are doing the speaking, to avoid staring uncomfortably at the person. People with low self-esteem, lacking confidence in themselves and their ability to communicate, will have very little eye contact. This lack of eye contact will create in others a feeling of suspicion and distrust. In his book *The Tell-Tale Eye*, E. Hess says the eyes may well give the most revealing and accurate of all human communication signals because they are a focal point on the body and the pupils work independently. When you see "eye to eye" with another person is when you have the basis for good communication.

Open Palms: The open palm is associated with truth, honesty, allegiance, and submission. In courts oaths are taken with the palm of the hand held in the air, and the palm is placed across the heart to demonstrate loyalty (such as when singing the National Anthem or saying the Pledge of Allegiance to the Flag). A sign of honesty and trustworthiness is seen when the palms are exposed in an open fashion. When the palm is hidden or turned face down, such as when pointing, there is an authoritarian image communicated. If the palm is closed into a fist, there is a feeling the speaker is trying to beat the listener into submission. Watch for the open palm gesture which says: I am being truthful and straightforward with you!

Leaning Forward: A slight leaning of the body toward the person talking suggests interest and attention being given. The forward lean should be done in a way not to invade the private territory of another (about 4-8 feet in a social setting). We normally lean the body toward anything we find interesting at the moment. In conversation, a leaning toward the individual communicates concern and a desire to hear every word.

Nodding of the Head: Nodding the head suggests one is listening and understanding. It does not necessary mean agreement. Constant nodding of the head, which can be annoying, may suggest the listener is actually tuning out.

The Vocabulary of Negative Body Language

Negative body language communicates a variety of things: tiredness, boredom, or other matters weighing on the person's mind.

Stiffness of the Body: Stiffness of the body may not only be seen in a rigid posture, but also in a wrinkled brow, jerky body motion, hands clasped in front or palms down on the table. These can reflect stress and disagreement or a form of anger.

Fidgeting: When a person is nervous, impatient, or bored, these are demonstrated by moving around a lot, playing with things, and drumming the fingers.

The following gestures suggest a negative or superior attitude.

Covering the Mouth: This gesture is often called the *mouth guard*. It can be seen in such moves as putting several fingers over the mouth or even a closed fist. Humphrey Bogart would often use this gesture in movies when his character was discussing criminal activities with other gangsters or when being questioned by the police. The meaning of this gesture is that some form of deceit is being perpetrated. But this is only the case if the person is speaking. If the person is listening to someone else speak and uses the mouth guard gesture, it means the person believes the speaker is lying or is deceitful.

Folding the Arms: As discussed above, this gesture suggests a closed-in attitude that is not willing to be open and straightforward.

Fingers in the Mouth: When under pressure there is a tendency to revert back to a childlike activity of sucking the thumb... it is seen in a gesture where the individual places one or more fingers in the mouth, cupping the palm under the jaw or chin. If this is not done, then the individual may put other objects in the mouth such as a pen or some other object. This response is a substitute for the thumb or the mother's breast, and it manifests an inner need for reassurance, but it can also suggest one is lying or being deceitful in some way. Be careful about drawing quick conclusions on these gestures.

International Gestures

Various cultures develop common gestures which usually convey the same message for everyone in those cultures. The following are some body languages that are spoken in other countries, which carry very different messages from those in America. These will be listed by country to make it easy to reference for those who might be traveling to these places.

Europe: Americans normally wave the whole hand (palm up, facing out) left to right to say hello or good bye. In Europe the correct way to wave hello or good bye is palm out, hand and arm stationary, fingers wagging up and down.

Peru: Raising the eyebrow means "money" or you must pay me money.

Taiwan: Blinking the eyes is very impolite.

Australia: It is considered improper to wink at a woman, even to express agreement or friendship. Also, a thumbs-up gesture, which normally means "okay" in most parts of the world, is considered a rude gesture.

Italy: A flicking of the ear means the gentleman is effeminate.

India: A sign of sincerity or remorse is signified by grasping the ear.

Colombia: Placing the classic "okay" sign (forefinger and thumb placed together to form a circle) over the nose signifies the person in question is gay.

Greece: Stroking the cheek means a person being viewed is attractive.

Latin America: The fingertip kiss means "beautiful!" and may be used for anything from women to wine or a new car. This gesture is also common in Europe. It probably originated from the religious custom of throwing kisses toward sacred objects such as statues and altars.

Netherlands: Making a circular motion around the side of the head means one has a telephone call. In Latin American, America, and Europe, this gesture means the person spoken of or viewed is crazy.

Bulgaria: To nod the head means "no." The same is true in Greece, but in other countries it means "yes."

Argentina: Tapping the head means: I'm thinking.

Paraguay: To tilt the head straight back means the person has just forgotten what he/she wanted to say. Crossing the fingers, a sign of good luck in America, is offensive.

African Countries: Holding the hands straight out with the index and little finger pointing out and the other fingers closed means an "evil eye" is being put on the person receiving the point.

Brazil: Holding the hands straight up with the index and little finger pointing up and the other fingers closed means a sign of good luck.

Far Eastern Countries: Using the finger(s) to motion someone toward you is considered an insult.

Germany/Greece/Russia/Brazil: The traditional American "okay" sign is considered either obscene or very impolite. In France it means worthless.

Indonesia: It is proper to use the thumb to point at someone. Pointing the index finger toward someone is considered impolite in most Middle and Far Eastern countries as well as in America.

Speaking With Handshakes

The tradition of shaking hands is ancient. It is believed the custom began from a gesture of holding the hands in the air to prove no weapons were being held in the hands. Eventually it developed into a friendly reach and grasp of the other's hand. In most English speaking countries, the gesture is a friendly way to say "hello" and "good bye." The handshake usually involves three to four pumps. There are several messages communicated through the handshake.

"I want to dominate you." This message is transmitted by a handshake in which the dominant person turns the other person's hand down and the dominant hand is in control. A study of several people in senior management positions revealed that 90 percent of them shook hands with a dominant handshake.

"I submit to you." This is the reverse. This individual offers the hand with the palm turned upward.

"I want your vote." This is sometimes called the politician's handshake. Both hands are used to smother the other person's hand. One hand is used for the shake, and the other hand is placed on the backside of the person's hand.

"I am stronger than you." Sometimes called the "knuckle grinder," this handshake is the trademark of an aggressive person who may tend to push others around.

"Don't get too close." This handshake holds the other person at a distance because the arm is thrust forward and kept straight. It is also called the "guided missile" because it begins a few feet away to insure there is no invading of the personal space.

"I'm not sure about you or me." This handshake is sometimes called the "dead fish." It is a limp handshake using only the fingers with little or no grip. It is also a gesture that says: keep your distance, I'm not sure I trust you. It is normally a sign of an insecure person who doesn't wish to affirm you because the person feels weak.

"You will really like me." This is also called the "jackhammer." The person grabs the hand and pumps it up and down several times with strong, affirmative pumps. The message is: I like you and you will like me, too.

"I need you on my committee." This is the handshake accompanied by the other hand which grabs the wrist, the elbow, the upper arm, or the shoulder. It is normally reserved for close friends, but is also used by politicians, salespeople, and committee chairs.

So what kind of handshake is acceptable? Here are some guidelines on how to shake hands with affirmation and confidence.

1. Be the first to extend the hand. This is true whether meeting a man or woman. Today it is acceptable for a man to extend his hand to the woman first.
2. Grasp the hand in a perpendicular (neither dormant nor submissive) motion, pumping three to four times.
3. Use the thumb to apply slight pressure to the back of the hand. A good firm grip that does not squeeze the other person's hand suggests a strong character and good self-esteem.
4. Protect the other person's territory by standing three to four feet away.

Working a Room

The information contained in this chapter provides some good guidelines to assist in communicating a strong, confident image to others. The next time you attend a social function you will be able to move around the room and study conversations. Even without hearing the words, you can determine what is happening in the conversation.

This information can also be used in various business settings such as job interviews, sales meetings, budget planning, corporate decision making, etc. As you sit at the conference table surveying each person and watching the clusters of body language that each uses, you will be able to read his/her sincerity, truthfulness, and openness.

However, it is also important for one to pay attention to the messages being sent personally. Crossing the arms in front of the body, slumping the shoulders, and failing to make good eye contact can communicate a weak, insecure person.

The human body is an incredible communication tool. When used positively, it can produce incredible results in convincing others to believe in you and respond positively to your words.

As a handy reference, here are some nonverbal behavior and possible interpretations:

Nonverbal	Meaning
Brisk, erect walk	Confidence
Standing with hands on hips	Readiness, aggression
Sitting with legs crossed, foot kicking slightly	Boredom
Arms crossed on chest	Defensiveness
Walking with hands in pockets, shoulders hunched	Dejection
Hand to cheek	Evaluation, thinking
Touching, slightly rubbing nose	Rejection, doubt, lying
Rubbing the eye	Doubt, disbelief
Hands clasped behind back	Anger, frustration, apprehension
Locked ankles	Apprehension
Head resting in hand, eyes downcast	Boredom
Rubbing the hands	Anticipation
Sitting with hands clasped behind head, legs crossed	Confidence, superiority
Open palm	Sincerity, openness, innocence
Pinching bridge of nose, eyes closed	Negative evaluation
Tapping or drumming fingers	Impatience

Nonverbal	Meaning
Steepling fingers	Authoritative
Patting/fondling hair	Lack of self-confidence, insecurity
Tilted head	Interest
Stroking chin	Trying to make a decision
Looking down, face turned away	Disbelief
Biting nails	Insecurity, nervousness
Pulling or tugging at ear	Indecision

Chapter 3
How to Communicate with an Appealing Personality

There are some people who do not believe they have a right to be heard or even appreciated. All of their lives they have lived in submission to the wishes and demands of others. They are only comfortable when yielding to the wishes of others. These people are called passive personalities.

Then there are those who push their way on to everyone they meet; or they push others around in order to get what they want. Their philosophy is we live in a dog-eat-dog world, and the Golden Rule means whoever has the gold rules! These people are called aggressive personalities.

A few individuals have discovered the secret of good human relations and communications. These people respect the rights of other while at the same time protecting their own rights. This attitude is a reflection of maturity and good self-esteem. These people are called assertive personalities.

To go passively through life inhibited, always allowing others to dominate and control, while holding desires inside, is a sign of low self-respect. The person who aggressively goes through life destroying others in order to get his/her own way also has feelings of low self-worth. The assertive persons who respect the rights of all people, including their own, have a proper view of self in relation to others. Their self-respect and self-esteem are positive.

Assertiveness/Passiveness/Aggressiveness

The assertive person is not pushy, selfish, or rude. Being assertive does not mean you will get your wants and wishes. Rather, to be assertive means to stand up for yourself, your beliefs, your opinions without demanding others support you or even agree with you.

The assertive person strives for win/win solutions to problems and disagreements. Win/win means each person in the negotiation or the argument comes away feeling respected and appreciated.

The aggressive person inappropriately expresses thoughts, feelings, and beliefs and consequently violates the rights of others. Passive-aggressive individuals do the same thing, but in a more subtle way, usually with a verbal outburst of anger after holding feelings inside for a while. Most aggressive people do not want a win/win, but rather strive for a win/lose solution. They win and others lose!

Passive behavior is more indirect allowing others to violate one's rights because of a lack of respect for one's own needs. The message it communicates is one of inferiority. The outcome is usually a lose/win situation because this individual does not respect his or her needs or rights. This person is a victim who feels devalued and humiliated and thus loses respect for the opinions and rights of others. If the passive person finally becomes aggressive, there will be feelings of guilt and frustration caused by the outburst of emotion and anger.

Most people operate in either a passive or aggressive mode. A few have discovered the power and confidence of assertiveness. A good definition of an assertive person is that he/she expresses needs, opinions, and beliefs because of a deep respect for self while at the same time respecting the basic rights of others and refusing to violate those rights. The assertive person respects self and others, regardless of their view, background, or belief system.

Assertive Characteristics

Strong Self-Esteem

The assertive person has reached a point in life in which self-esteem is strong enough for the individual to feel confident enough to express thoughts and ideas without fear of consequences. This type of self-esteem usually begins in the early, formative years when the young person realizes it is okay to have a personal opinion or belief and not fear expressing it. This type of home environment is one in which the parents or guardians do not believe there is one right answer or one best way of doing something. The ideas of others, the opinions of those who see things differently, are respected. In this type of environment the young person does not fear disagreeing, but is in fact encouraged to think on his/her own and is also respected for ideas that may be opposite of the parents or guardians.

Clear Values

An assertive person is one who has been trained to think through complex issues and come to conclusions in which certain values are held. A person whose values have been handed down from parents/guardians or from the community in general may feel the values are either not worth defending, or that the values being held are for all time and all people; therefore, any disagreement will result in an effort to force conformity or reject the person(s) holding the opposing values. Either response, obviously, is not acceptable. Once a person comes to a point of holding a particular value as a result of careful research and reflection, that person should feel it is his/her right to articulate that value while respecting those who do not hold the same value. It is obvious that strong self-esteem and critical thinking go hand in hand.

Communication Skills

A third characteristic of an assertive person is good communication skills. These would involve such things as clear, articulate expression of thought; strong, positive body language; and active listening skills. Before you seek to be understood, it is important to understand others first. This involves listening carefully, asking questions to clarify understanding, watching the body language, and feeding back their thoughts and feelings in order to fully comprehend their thought process. In this way you are able to communicate your interest in and respect for what the other person says and believes. After this, you have earned the right to express your own thoughts and belief system.

Assertiveness in Confrontation

Arguments and disagreements among individuals are as old as the human race.

How does an assertive person handle confrontations? The following are skills the assertive person will use in situations where there are differences of opinion:

"I" Messages

There are three components to "I" messages: behavior (action), feelings (response to action), and effect (result of action). "I" messages do not accuse others by using the pronoun "you." By using "I" messages, you are able to communicate accurately and precisely, without blaming the other person. Here is an example: "When people raise their voice at me (behavior) I feel threatened (feelings) and cannot really hear what they are trying to say (effect)." As you can see, this is much better than stuffing the feelings or blowing up in anger and frustration. It is also a better approach than saying: "You make me so angry when you raise your voice." Notice how the "you" message accuses and blames the other person for the behavior. That type of statement will only escalate the argument and add fuel to the anger.

In addition, some will choose "it" and "we" statements to cloud their real feelings. Here are some examples in which you will be able to see the difference between "I" and "it"/"we" statements.

- "It upsets me when you don't call."
- "When you don't call, I become worried and upset."
- "It's nice to be with you."
- "When we're together, I feel peaceful and relaxed."
- "It was a boring meeting."
- "The meeting was long and I was bored."
- "We need to make some changes here."
- "I need to make some changes here."
- "We ought to buy more paper."

- "I ought to buy more paper."

There are also a couple of "eraser words" which we should remove from our conversations; they are "but" and "however." Here's how they are often used.

- "You are a nice person, but . . . ."
- "The report you turned in was fine; however, ..."

When these words are used in conversation, they erase everything that was said before them.

"Fogging"

There is a technique in martial arts (primarily in jiu-jitsu) that emphasizes a "yielding" technique which redirects an opponent's momentum so that in effect he defeats himself. Fogging is similar to jiu-jitsu in that its power is in the yielding. Think of an angry person in terms of that person trying to climb a mountain. If the person is interrupted on the way up, the anger has not subsided, it is only been diverted momentarily. The angry person has to get to the top of the mountain, so to speak, in order to get out all the anger. Once the person begins descending on the other side of the mountain of anger, you are in a better position to communicate with him or her. As the person climbs the mountain, imagine the mountain is enveloped with fog, and the higher the person climbs, the more fog the person encounters. The fog is your "yielding."

The yielding (fogging) principle creates a diffusing of the other person's attack by *accepting* whatever the person says to you without rebuttal. Fogging is an assertive skill that does not necessarily agree with the criticism or blame the person is putting on you, but rather allows the person to get it all out (in other words, reach the top of the mountain), so the anger will subside. Fogging acknowledges the other person has a right to feel the way he or she feels, without agreeing with the accusations, criticisms, etc. The technique of fogging allows you to listen carefully to what is being said and discover some validity in the remarks.

In professional counseling this is called Reflective Listening. It is the art or skill of allowing the other person to say what is on his or her mind without interruption. It also involves what is called Rephrasing or Empathy statements. This is the feedback the "fogger" gives to the other person which verifies the feelings and acknowledges the fact that what has been said has been heard. An example of this technique may be heard in a discussion between two people, one who is very angry about something the other person has done. So the "Accuser" blames the "Fogger" for what has happened, and the "Fogger" responds with these types of comments:

Accuser: "You were supposed to call me yesterday about the Simmon's Contract. Why didn't you?"

Fogger: "I know that my failure to call has upset you."

Accuser: "It was very inconsiderate of you to keep me waiting by the phone all day."

Fogger: "That's true, I should be more considerate of your time."

Accuser: "This is not the only time this has happened. You have done this before."

Fogger: "Yes, I'm sure I have, and I certainly would not want to be treated that way."

Accuser: "Then why did you not call me?"

Fogger: "I knew you needed that information, but my day was full and I simply did not have time to explain in complete detail all the information you needed about the contract. I should have called you and set up another appointment. The next time, I will be more considerate."

Notice that the reason for not making the telephone call was eventually given, but only after the Accuser has been able to get out the anger and finally come to the point of asking for the reason. Until that point, any reason would have been only an excuse. But at this point, after the Fogger has acknowledged the Accuser's feelings and agreed with the Accuser there is some legitimacy to the argument, the Accuser will be in a better position to listen to reason.

The important thing about fogging is that the person who is angry needs to keep talking until he/she reaches "the top of the mountain" and the anger starts subsiding. Until that happens, any response of defensiveness or argumentation will only result in an escalated confrontation. Fogging operates on the principle: absorption is dispersion, victory is defeat. Any professional boxer who has mastered the skill of boxing will tell you it is always best to take a punch and allow the body to absorb it by moving in the same direction as the punch is going. It will weaken the force of impact. In fogging, the person receiving the "punch" is not giving in, but is allowing the other person to use up all the "energy" or strength of argument so resolution can be obtained; therefore, the fogger is always in control of the confrontation, although at times it may appear the other person is "winning." For those aggressive people who view confrontation as battle, this technique obviously will not be considered. But for the assertive person who keeps in mind the end goal of diffusing the aggression, the result will be extremely rewarding.

Remember that an aggressive person needs resistance in order to continue the aggression. If there is no resistance, aggression will eventually be defused. The assertive person has the courage and self-confidence to allow the anger and aggression to be given enough credence to eventually become ineffective.

There are two more skills that enhance the fogging technique making it a more effective technique:

Negative Inquiry

Negative Inquiry is the ability to pursue a criticism or complaint to discover more about how the individual feels about you. It is a pinpointing technique that helps you understand the *real* problem that is bothering the critic. For example, instead of saying, "You are right, I really fouled up on that one . . . ." It would be even better to say, "You know, you are probably right about that. What do you think I might have done to avoid that situation?" This type of open-ended question will help both parties reach a mutual conclusion that each can benefit from either by understanding the situation better, or agreeing on an alternative solution. In addition, there is also another useful technique.

Negative Assertion

Use this technique when you've made a mistake and you have to admit something that is uncomfortable. In fact, what you have to do is separate yourself from your actions in the mind of the other person. This is an especially difficult thing to do when a person wants to be right all the time. But the way it works is simply to say: "I was wrong. I'm sorry. I'll learn from this and do better the next time." This is a skill that has to be developed because most people find it extremely difficult to acknowledge shortcomings. When you fail to admit what others obviously know is true about you, this failure lowers their esteem of you and creates distrust in their minds. This is another form of fogging, absorbing the wrong and moving on.

Assertiveness Begins With Equality

The key to assertive behavior is realizing your equality with all other people. This, of course, does not mean you are as talented as some others might be, or that you are as smart, as pretty, as athletic. But on a human level, no one is superior to you and no one is inferior to you. Your human rights come about, not on the basis of race, color, nationality, etc., but simply because you are one of several billion human beings living on the face of the earth with whom you share total and absolute equality.

No one has a right to look down on another person, regardless of that person's place in life. Just because someone is less educated, or less athletic, or lives in a certain "part" of town does not make that person inferior to anyone. The same is true if a person is better educated, or more athletic ... or if the person lives in another "part" of town; the person is not superior in any way to another human being. The assertive person respects the fact that all people are created equal and deserve respect and honor. But the assertive person goes beyond just the words and actually treats others with the dignity they deserve.

The assertive person realizes that others will react based on the way the assertive person comes across to them. If there is no respect shown, there will be no respect received; if there is no honor given, there will be no honor received. Thus assertive behavior is like all other behavior; it becomes a mirror that reflects certain images onto others, and their behavior becomes a mirror reflecting certain images back. Usually the images reflected back are similar to the ones received!

Positive Self-Talk

Another important aspect of assertive behavior is how we talk to ourselves. Everyone talks to himself or herself. Self-talk is the thoughts we think from the time we wake up until the time we go to sleep. Perhaps dreams could also be described in some respect as self-talk, because they are the result of frustrations and unresolved issues which linger in our lives. In our dreams we are trying to resolve those issues or in some way bring closure to those unsolved problems. So we can say that self-talk is continuous. Unfortunately, most of what we say to ourselves about the world we live in is negative. This is especially true in regard to what we say about ourselves.

The passive person will say:

- "No one cares about hearing my ideas."
- "I'm not important."
- "If I speak up, I'll probably look stupid."
- "I'm not sure I can."

The aggressive person will say:

- "No one cares about anyone else, so you've gotta look out for number one!"
- "I don't really care what you think."
- "Why can't you learn to do it right!"
- "You make me so angry."

The assertive person will say:

- "I respect the opinions of others."
- "I care about what you think and how you feel."

Communication Skills for the 21st Century

- "I don't want to hurt you, even though I don't agree with you."
- "I am a valuable person and so are you."
- "My opinions count, too."

Our thoughts always come before our feelings. The way we think about things forms our perceptions; our perceptions shape our attitudes, which affect our feelings and emotions, which are then expressed in behavior. If this process is negative, the result will often be conflict with others; if the process is positive, the result will be cooperation with others. It all begins with how we think!

How To Begin

Okay, you say, I want to begin, so what do I do . . . go to bed tonight and wake up tomorrow saying: "I am an assertive person"? Of course the answer is no. But here are some good guidelines that will get you started on the road to assertive living.

1. Monitor your behavior. Do you speak up and express yourself when you feel it is important to do so? Do you stand up for yourself while respecting the feelings and opinions of others? Do you feel good about yourself and do you believe you are a person of worth whose ideas and opinions count in the arena of public opinion? Check yourself at the end of each day to see how assertively you have lived that day. Make mental notes of those areas that need improvement.

2. Keep a journal. Many people have found great value in journaling. This can be especially helpful in keeping a consistent record of your assertive behavior vs. your passive or aggressive behavior. Don't forget to write down observations about your body language and the body language of others—things such as eye contact, posture, gestures (open or closed, arms folded across chest), facial expressions, etc. Remember, body language communicates 55 percent of the message!

3. Set some goals. It is helpful not only to set goals mentally, but also to write them down so you can see them. Written goals become more realistic once they can be seen on paper. Be sure to start small and move up in increments so when there are setbacks (and there will be!), you won't feel too discouraged. You may want to begin with your family relationships or your friends and then move into the work place, from there into a broader social arena, and perhaps into the community. You can take the goals as far as you desire. Once you begin to have success reaching those goals and seeing how people respond to you, your self-esteem will become stronger and your goals will grow larger.

4. Center on a particular person. Set your sights on one person who is difficult for you to get along with on a regular basis. In your mind, visualize past conversations and think of how you might have responded differently. Think of words or phrases you could have used to be more assertive and still have shown proper respect. Replay those situations and conversations until you feel comfortable with the way you see yourself handling them. Then think of what future encounters might be like. Imagine those same types of conversations; take a pen and paper and write down what you plan to say the next time. This is an excellent way to rehearse assertive behavior and make it a part of your daily life.

5. Find some role models. If you know anyone who is an assertive person, watch his or her behavior and try to model the things you see that seem to work in a positive way. If you know the person well enough, set up a luncheon or some other appointment and get ideas from them that will help you.

6. Think positively. You will experience setbacks. No one is perfectly assertive in every way. It is a type of behavior that one grows in and learns every day. So there will be days in which you take one step forward and two steps backward. Those are the times you will need to think

positively about yourself and others. Otherwise, you will find yourself falling back into the "doom loops," the old patterns of behavior and negative thinking.

7. Give yourself time. Changes of behavior do not take place overnight. You will need time. So be patient with yourself and give yourself rewards when you've done well and review and learn when you fail. Over time you will discover a marvelous transformation taking place in your life and in the way others respond to you. Your self-esteem and self-confidence will grow by leaps and bounds!

Anger And Assertiveness

Anger is an emphatic message: Pay attention to me! I don't like what you are doing! You are in my way! Give me justice! Anger is characterized primarily by fear. As a matter of fact, it originates in fear, the fear of losing, or of being hurt, or of hindrance from reaching a goal, or fear of lowered self-esteem. In some way or another, anger is an expression of fear.

When anger is combined with stress, they produce in the body what is called the flight or fight response. The flight or fight response contains the following physical characteristics:

- Increased heart rate
- Sweaty palms
- Rise in blood pressure
- Tense muscles in shoulder and neck area
- Upset stomach
- Headache

All of these are a result of how you label an event and the response you take toward the event. Anger and aggressive behavior can have devastating impact on your immune system and eventually your long-term health.

So how does an assertive person deal with stressful and fearful situations that can arouse anger? Glad you asked. Here are some suggestions:

How to Communicate with an Appealing Personality

1. When in a difficult setting that is causing anger to increase, be sure to listen attentively without agreement and interruption. When the other person stops talking, allow two or three seconds before saying anything to be sure all of the other person's thoughts are completed. If you are not clear, ask for clarification with a statement such as: "Help me to understand what you are thinking, are you saying . . . ."
2. Acknowledge the other person's thoughts and feelings with statements such as: "I can see how you could feel that way." "Thank you for telling me how you feel." "I know this must be upsetting to you."
3. Avoid accusing the other person. "You" language always accuses others. So be careful about such statements as: "You make me so angry." or "You always do such and such."
4. Then state your thoughts and ideas. Be sure to use "I" language when stating your position: "I see how that could make you angry, here's how I see the problem . . . ."
5. Address behavior first, followed by the effect, and then the outcome. Here is an example: "When my telephone calls are not returned (behavior), that creates stress (effect) because I cannot proceed without the information (outcome).

The assertive person learns how to keep the lid on in stressful situations when expressing thoughts, feelings, and emotions and, at the same time, respecting the other person's thoughts, feelings, and emotions. So the assertive person has the strength of character to respect his/her own feelings and thoughts and then show the same respect to others. This strength of character will enable everyone to be a better communicator in any environment.

Chapter 4

How to Communicate with a Professional Writing Style

Writing systems, consisting of marks made for counting or identification, date back 30,000 years, but full writing systems have developed only during the past 5,000 years.

Writing systems have made possible the technological advances that have taken humanity from hunting, gathering, and simple farming to the exploration of space. Writing created a permanent record of knowledge so a fund of information could accumulate from one generation to another. Before the time of writing, human knowledge was limited to memory—what one could learn for oneself or find out from talking to others. Writing extended the geography of communication. It allowed accurate communication at a distance without traveling or relying on the memory of a messenger.

The First Alphabet

The Greeks probably borrowed their writing system from the Arabs, Aramaeans, Hebrews, or Phoenicians sometime around the ninth century BC. The Greeks divided the consonants from the vowels and wrote each separately. The results were called an alphabet, from the names of the first Greek letters, *alpha* and *beta*. The Greeks, therefore, did what no other civilization before or since has done: invented the alphabet! All subsequent alphabets, ancient or modern, derive from the Greek alphabet.

Modern Writing

The evolution of English writing has resulted in a sophisticated system of communication using words, phrases, punctuation, paragraphs, numbers, units of measure, equations, symbols, grammar, abbreviation, and capitalization. When these items are used effectively, communication of ideas from one person to others is accomplished. The purpose of this chapter is to give some basic guidelines for professional writing.

The Most Important Key

Communicators often overlook the most important key to excellent writing: the reader. The fact is, no one has to read what you write even if is an important document that contains information needed by the reader. The reader may tell you the document was read, but you discover later that important details were not followed. So what can be done in order to write a document that not only will be read, but also will be understood and followed explicitly? The answer is simple: The reader must believe the document was for him or her *personally*.

In order to be a reader-centered writer, there are several questions you must keep in mind about the reader/s:

- How old are they?
- What is their job? What were their previous jobs?
- What upsets them?
- What are their hobbies?
- What do they want at home/on the job?
- How much do they know about the topic you are writing about?
- Do they have some reason not to read what you write?
- How will your ideas help them?
- What is your relationship to them? Do they have any reason to resent that relationship?
- Do they have a reason to refuse to accept your ideas?
- Why will they want to read this document?

Granted, many of these questions may not have answers, but just thinking about a list such as this one can give you a basis to address issues that will be of interest to the reader.

As you begin writing your document, you will start to anticipate the reader's reactions. Questions the reader may have will come to mind, and you will be able to answer them in advance. You will begin to write in the form of a conversation with the reader as you anticipate questions, comments, objections, etc.

Before long, you will discover you are writing for the ear, not the eye. This is characteristic of all good writers. Your writing will soon take on a natural rhythm, and artificial phrases will disappear from your vocabulary. Those phrases will be replaced with such things as contractions (it's, I'll, you'll, won't, can't, couldn't, etc.), questions ("How does that sound?"), direct addresses ("Joe, when can you get back with me?"), even sentence fragments ("Looks good.").

As your style becomes more natural, you will want to develop your *sixth sense* in writing. Your intuition will tell you how to explain things to the reader so he or she can *see* what you see. You will begin to sense the reader's questions, confusion, worries, curiosities, longings, etc. Then you will begin to describe things more clearly using concrete language. You will describe how things and people feel: rough, smooth, soft, hard, heavy, sad, happy, angry, etc. Before long you will add color to your descriptions, then shapes and designs. Then you will learn how to describe sounds, such as a rushing river that sounds like an approaching locomotive. When your writing reaches this level of professionalism, your readers will look forward to receiving your letters, memos, reports, etc.

Let Your Writing Flow

Start listening to your writing by reading it out loud. Your ear will begin to catch some of the glitches that your eyes miss. Here is an example of a sentence that, when read out loud, reveals the fact it is too long and somewhat confusing:

> In the interest of increasing traffic to our corporate Web site, and to garner greater market share in internet sales at our electronic storefront and retail sites, we will be organizing a comprehensive mailing list of prospective and current clients.

If you read that out loud, your ear caught the difficulty of the structure and the confusion of the phrases. Let's do a rewrite:

> We will organize a comprehensive mailing list of prospective and current clients in the interest of:
> 1. Increasing traffic to our corporate Web site.
> 2. Increasing both our electronic and retail market share.

Top-Down Writing

A second characteristic of excellent writing is what I call *top-down writing*. The idea is to get to the main point in the first paragraph. This is opposite of what most of us were taught in school. Almost all writing classes taught us to present our data first and then draw conclusions based on the evidence. The result of this style of communication is we tend to bury our main point deep into our document, sometimes at the very end, the last sentence in the last paragraph. Modern writing has taken on a whole new approach, and that approach is to present the main idea in the first sentence or two in the first paragraph.

A reader-centered writer realizes that the reader can fall asleep trying to find the main point in the document. So if you want to be a great communicator, put your message first. Here is an excellent example of how not to do top-down writing:

> Since the invention of movable type, there have been collectors of books. Here at the Company Library, we have been privileged to inherit the collections of many rare spirits. Our technology trove is world renowned. We take great pride in our periodical file. But alas, the financial problems of our conglomerate have spread to our door, and we are now faced with an enormous deficit. If that deficit is not soon made up, we may be forced to close the library, depriving hundreds of employees of a major resource.

Here is how top-down writing would rewrite the above:

> To keep the Company Library from closing, we need you to approve the enclosed authorization for an extra $100,000 above

budget by June 1. Otherwise we'll have to sell off the contents in June. The reasons are... ." (Jonathan Price, *Put That in Writing,* pp.18,19).

One of the ways to guarantee you get to the point first is to do some brainstorming on your document before the writing project begins. Take a blank sheet of paper, write the subject or topic in the middle of the paper, and draw a circle around it. Then draw lines out in all directions and put circles at the ends of these lines. In the circles, write down examples of subjects, ideas, thoughts, points which you want to make in your document. Then draw more lines and circles from these points and jot down any subpoints. This exercise is called mind-mapping.

Once you have put down on paper all the ideas you can think of, organize them in order of importance. Then write down one main point that summarizes all these ideas. Now you have the main message with which you will begin writing your document.

This type of brainstorming prevents preorganization. Most of us will begin our brainstorming by outlining our material as we think of each point or idea. The problem with this style of writing is the sequence is often out of order and the main idea is lost somewhere deep in the document. Mind mapping is a technique of brainstorming that allows you to get all your ideas down on paper first, then you can organize them in the order that seems most logical with the main thought at the very beginning.

Active Voice

Another important technique of good writing is active voice writing. Active verbs give muscle and action to your sentences. Passive verbs just announce states of being: I am; it was; they were; we are; it will be; they have been; it might have been; it had been; it would have been; they are being. When any form of the verb *to be* is used, there is no action, no responsibility. Here is an example:

Passive voice:

> The store has been closed this week while the plumbing is being repaired.

Active voice:

> We closed the store while the plumbers repair the leaks.

When active voice verbs are used, the sentences are clearer and shorter. Passive writing hides the one performing the action. Many writers use the passive because the active seems to be more direct. There are times when you may want to soften the impact of a statement. An example might be a written performance review in which you do not want to be too direct. So instead of writing:

> You will make the following corrections...

A gentler way may be to write:

> The following corrections should be made soon...

However, in most cases the active voice is the preferable way to write.

There is an easy technique to move sentences out of the passive to the active. Just look carefully at your sentences and ask yourself where the *actor* is. Each sentence must have an actor, that is, the person or thing performing the action. Once the *actor* is found, move it to the front of the sentence. Your sentence will thus become active. Here is a simple illustration:

> The job was performed by the workmen.

The *actor* of the sentence is the workmen. So move the *actor* to the front of the sentence:

> The workmen performed the job.

It is not necessary to make every single sentence an active voice, but an effort should be made to at least begin most paragraphs with active sentences. You will draw the reader into the paragraph by a strong and clear active sentence, and your writing will take on a more professional style. So when you have finished a document, take a moment and read each sentence to see if it might be better written in the active voice. This one technique can make your documents more powerful means of communication.

Eliminate Wordiness—Prune and Sharpen

Top-notch writers know it is important to make their points with the fewest possible words. They strive to write clearly, eliminating jargon and wordiness. Special effort is given to avoid phrases that contain too many words. The fewer words used to convey the same idea, the better the writing will be. For example:

Acceptable: I need your help *in order* to complete this project.

Better: I need your help to complete this project.

Acceptable: Due to the fact that the order was delayed, we were unable to finish the project.

Better: Because the order was delayed, we were unable to finish the project.

Even better: We're unable to finish the project because the order was delayed.

Acceptable: It is our opinion that the contract should be renewed.

Better: We believe the contract should be renewed.

Here is a list of wordy phrases with replacement words or phrases:

at a latter date	later
despite the fact that	although
due to the fact that	because
for the purpose of	for, to
in addition	also
in a number of cases	some
in order that	so
in order to	to
in reference to	about

Communication Skills for the 21st Century

in terms of	as for
in the amount of	for, of
in the event of	if
in the near future	soon
in this day and age	now, today
in this regard	(delete)
in view of	because, since
it is our opinion that	we believe
on the occasion of	when
prior to	before
subsequent to	after
without further delay	immediately
with reference to	about
with respect to	about
would you please be so kind as to	please
a large number of	many
along the lines	like
as a general rule	generally
as yet	yet
at all times	always
at your earliest convenience	now, soon
be considered as	is
by means of	by
despite the fact that	although, even though
during the course of	during
even more significant	more significant
exhibits the ability	can
has been widely	is acknowledged as

has proved itself to be	has proved, is
have discussion of	discuss
hold a meeting	meet
inasmuch as	since
in many cases	often
in some cases	sometimes
in the course of	during, while
in the majority of instances	usually, generally
in the vicinity of	near
is equipped with	has, contains
it is clear that	clearly
on a daily basis	daily
on weekly basis	weekly
on an annual basis	yearly
on the basis of	by, from
prior to that time	before
start off	start
take action	act
the reason why is that	because
until such time as	until
with reference to	about
with the result that	so that

In addition to these wordy phrases, there are redundant phrases that should be avoided as well.

Redundant: In the month of September our retail sales soared.

Better: In September our retail sales soared.

Redundant: Hayes and Yates is the one and only source of the material.

Better: Hayes and Yates is the only source of the material.

Redundant: I have enclosed a check for the amount of $44.44.
Better: I enclosed a check for $44.44.
A few redundant phrases are:

and etc.	etc.
completely perfect	perfect
consensus of opinion	consensus
each and every	each
first and foremost	first
follows after	follows
full and complete	full or complete
general consensus	consensus
honest and open	honest
if and when	if or when
very unique	unique
one and only	only
meet together	meet
willing and eager	willing or eager

In addition to the above, there is also the problem with jargon. Technical writers tend to use jargon excessively. Jargon consists of long words usually ending in -ize, -tion, -ity.

Readers are often confused because the words or phrases are difficult to read and comprehend. Here are some examples from *Office Guide to Business Letters, Memos, & Reports*, pp. 4,5:

Jargon: An enhanced commitment to a public relations effort remains a viable option for the firm.

Better: We may also wish to improve our public relations.

Jargon: The implementation of cost-cutting strategies can impact budgetary deficits.

Better: Cutting costs will reduce deficits.

Other examples of jargon are:
- acknowledge receipt of
- answer affirmatively, negatively
- expend maximum effort
- feedback
- impact a problem
- input
- interface
- proactive
- remunerate

Now add to this list some clichés, phrases which have lost their meaning over the years because of overuse.
- allow me to
- along these lines
- down but not out
- fact of life
- keep abreast
- last but not least
- meet the eye
- nip in the bud
- over the hill
- pave the way
- slow but sure
- to be perfectly honest
- work like a dog

Let's take an example of business writing and see how we may cut out the fluff to get at its substance. Here is the sentence:

> Over the past quarter our company has taken action on the issue of customer service and has initiated advance planning in the area of return policies.

Now let's rewrite this sentence and reduce the words and tie the two clauses more closely together by replacing "and" with "by." Here's how it should read:

> During the last quarter our company has focused on customer service by developing new return policies.

Notice the total number of words were reduced from 26 to 16. Here is another way to write the sentence with an active voice style:

> Our company focused last quarter on customer service by developing new return policies.

That rewrite reduced the sentence down to 13 words and gave more power to the overall style of writing.

Gender-Free Writing

A very important development has taken place in business writing during the past few years; it is called *gender-free writing*. There are certain words and phrases which are viewed as "prejudiced" to some readers. Even though you do not intend for them to be viewed that way; nevertheless, it is important to make a special effort to avoid them. A very important part of being reader-centered is being sure you do not write things that can hurt, anger, or offend your audience.

Keep in mind that many of our masculine phrases come from stereotypes held by Northern Europe many centuries ago. Thus the language of our culture causes us to discriminate in ways that may not be intended. So read over your material to be sure you have not offended anyone in any way.

Here are some examples of words and phrases one should pay attention to carefully to prevent offending the reader; suggested alternatives are given:

Mankind	People, or human beings

Manmade	Synthetic
Manpower	Workforce
Straight with us	Honest with us
That's white of you	That's generous
Chairman	Chair or chairperson
Policeman	Police officer
Foreman	Supervisor
Postman	Mail carrier
Waitress	Server
Stewardess	Flight attendant

Another very important part of sensitivity writing is avoiding the masculine pronoun.

Example: Everyone should pick up *his* coat at the door.

Instead:

You can pick up your coat at the door.

All persons should pick up their coats at the door.

Everyone should pick up his/her coat at the door.

Give the Reader Air

It is important for your document to appear reader friendly. If the "look" of your document appears open (with plenty of white space) and friendly, the reader is more likely to take the time to read it carefully. A cluttered letter, memo, or report tends to discourage the reader as soon as it is opened.

Here are some suggestions that will guarantee a layout that engages the reader.

Use Short Paragraphs

The old rule on paragraph change was that one should not change paragraph unless there was a change of subject, topic, or thought. That rule has led to long, boring paragraphs that discourage readers immediately upon looking at the document. Here is a better guideline: Change paragraphs about every five or six sentences. The fact is, almost every sentence contains a thought, topic, or subject. So use your judgment about changing each paragraph. Before long you will get a *feel* for shorter, sharper paragraphs.

Use Headlines

A headline is a title or label to a paragraph. A headline helps the reader understand the paragraph better because the subject of the paragraph is in the headline. Here are some tips on the layout of headlines:

- Put more space above the headline than below it, so it will stand out and the reader will know it belongs to the paragraph below.
- Be sure the headline is appropriate to the paragraph and is clear and understandable to the reader.
- Multiple paragraphs may be used beneath each headline, or you may choose to have only one paragraph.

Use Bullets and Lists

Bullets and lists organize the material so the reader can scan over the list of items, names, etc., and not waste time trying to separate each item from the others as it appears in the paragraph. If the list has a sequence or order, it is a good idea to number them. Bullets can be numbered or symbols can be used as well. It is not necessary to punctuate the bullets or lists unless you use full sentences or paragraphs.

Go the Extra Mile

The above suggestions will provide a framework for your letters, reports, memos, etc. The idea behind all these suggestions is to do a little extra work to save your reader time, which will result in a better response from him/her, greater respect for you, and a saving of your time so you will not have to go back over the same material again.

You should think of every document you write as a sales presentation. You want to sell your idea, plan, proposal, etc. So make it as clear and understandable as possible, always keeping in mind how the reader may respond to it. The skill you develop in this approach will pay many dividends!

Joseph Pulitzer once said, "Put it before them briefly so they will read it, clearly so they will appreciate it, picturesquely so they will remember it and, above all, accurately so they will be guided by its light." The four words in the above quote which describe good writing are *briefly, clearly, picturesquely,* and *accurately.*

This chapter can be summarized with the seven C's of professional style:

Conversational: Write the way you speak, for the ear not the eye!

Clear: Adapt to each reader so what you write will be clear and understandable to that particular person.

Concise: Eliminate unnecessary words.

Complete: Be sure it has all the information which you want to communicate to the reader.

Concrete: Write about the things people can see, smell, taste, touch, hear, count, or do.

Constructive: From the beginning to the end, set a positive tone. Even when writing negative thoughts, think of how they can be expressed in a positive, encouraging way.

Correct: Be sure your grammar, structure of sentences, and spelling are all correct in order to reflect the professionalism which should characterize your writing.

Chapter 5

How to Communicate with Proper Grammar

"I don't need none," shouted the lady of the house even before the young man at the door had a chance to say anything. "How do you know, lady?" he said. "I just might be selling grammar books."

If you do not see the humor in the above joke, you need to study this chapter closely. Do you find yourself becoming frustrated with such issues as whether to use *imply* or *infer*? Can you never decide if it is *effect* or *affect*? Do you question yourself when you say . . . *for my friend and me*?

If you are an average English-speaking person, these and many other questions often disturb you, causing feelings of insecurity when you speak or write.

English is the most widely spoken language in the world. It has been estimated that about one out of every six human beings around the globe speaks English. It has become the universally accepted language of international communications. Over eighty percent of the world's computer programs are in English. More than half of the newspapers around the world are published in English. Close to sixty-five percent of the world's radio programs are in English. Even nations that have their own languages are teaching English as a second language (China, for example, with over two hundred fifty million).

English now has the largest vocabulary of all the world's languages. Some estimate there are over two million words in the English language. The majority of international phone calls are made in English; over seventy percent of international mail is written and addressed in English.

The human race has never had a language that has grown so large and produced so much literature. It is predicted that very soon English will be the universal, international language for our "global village." It behooves each of us, therefore, to not only realize the beauty and power of our language, but also to write and speak it correctly. This chapter will assist you with these goals.

The Basics

The English language, with its hundreds of thousands of words, has only eight groups or classes for all those words: nouns, pronouns, verbs, adjectives, adverbs, prepositions, conjunctions, and interjections.

A noun gives a name to something, such as a person, an animal, a place, or an object. There are also names for substances, qualities, actions, and measures of time or quantity. There are five categories of nouns: common (e.g., desk), proper (e.g., City Hall), collective (e.g., family), concrete (e.g., computer), abstract (e.g., faith).

A pronoun takes the place of a noun or another pronoun. If, for example, you don't want to say the person's name more than once, you can refer to him or her. If you don't won't to refer to an object more than once, then the word you would use in place of the object is "it." A list of pronouns is given below for a handy reference:

I	she	this	several
my	her	that	other
mine	hers	these	another
me	it	those	anybody
we	its	all	everybody
our	they	any	nobody
ours	their	both	somebody
us	theirs	each	no one
You	them	either	someone
yours	which	neither	everyone

your	what	few	one
he	who	many	whoever
his	whose	none	whosoever
him	whom	some	anyone

A verb is a word that shows action, being, or state of being. A verb shows what something has, does, or is. A verb is the only part of speech that can make a statement about the subject. For example: *The car hit the tree.* The verb is "hit." Without the verb, the sentence would read: *The car the tree.* The verb tells what the car did to the tree. When a verb is put in a sentence, the sentence usually becomes a complete thought.

Adjectives identify, number, and describe (or in some way tell about) nouns and pronouns. They answer these questions: Which one? What kind? How many? How much? Articles such as *a an the* are also considered adjectives (*A* precedes words starting with consonants; *An* precedes words starting with vowels or vowel sounds: *a* record, *a* woman, *an* army, *an* honor, *an* invitation).

Adverbs tell about the main verb or even a complete sentence. Adverbs also describe adjectives and other adverbs. Adverbs usually answer questions such as: How? Why? When? Where? To what extent? Most adverbs end in -ly. Here is a sample list:

firmly	sharply	not
blatantly	carefully	too
briskly	soon	there
candidly	sometimes	more
bitterly	here	now
daily	very	when
Approximately	well	why
mistakenly	where	quite

Prepositions show relationship between certain words in a sentence. Prepositions before nouns and pronouns show the relationship of the nouns or pronouns and some other word in the sentence. For example: We have a box *for* the camera. The word *for* is a preposition which shows the relationship of box to camera. The wreck happened *near* the airport. The preposition *near* shows the relationship of the wreck to the airport. Here is a handy list of prepositions:

about	over	with
among	beyond	near
of	past	underneath
under	unto	within
without	against	to
during	for	across
Through	in	against
above	into	since
by	down	along
beside	since	around
off	upon	onto
until	at	before
beneath	on	behind
between	after	besides
from	toward	out
up	like	inside

The word *conjunction* comes from two Latin words which mean to *join with* or to *join together*. So conjunctions are connecting words. They connect words, phrases, and clauses. There are three basic types of conjunctions: coordinate conjunctions (and, but, or, for, nor, so, yet), subordinate conjunctions (although, as, as long as, as soon as, as if, if, before, how, in order that, inasmuch as, so that, than, until, till, unless, when, whereas, whether, while, why, after, since, because), and correlative conjunctions (either/or, neither/nor, both/and, whether/or, whether/if, not only/but also).

The final part of speech is called an interjection. Interjections show strong feeling or emotion. They are words such as: *Oh! Wow! Alas! Hey! Bah! Pshaw!*

These eight parts of speech are described rather well in the poem: *Grammar In Rhyme* (author unknown):

> A noun's the name of anything,
> As *school* or *garden*, *hoop* or *swing*.
>
> Adjectives tell the kind of noun;
> as *great, small, pretty, white,* or *brown*.
>
> Instead of nouns the pronouns stand:
> *Their* heads, *your* face, *its* paw, *his* hand.
>
> Verbs tell of something being done:
> You *read, count, sing, laugh, jump,* or *run*.
>
> How things are done the adverbs tell;
> As *slowly, quickly, ill,* or *well*.
>
> Conjunctions join the words together;
> As men *and* women, wind *or* weather.
>
> The preposition stands before
> A noun; as *in* or *through* a door.
>
> The interjection shows surprise;
> As *Oh*! how pretty! *Ah*! how wise!

Where it All Begins

When the above parts of speech are put together to express a **complete thought**, it is called a *sentence*. There are three basic parts to a sentence: a subject, a verb, a complete idea (a thought that makes sense on its own). A sentence can actually have only one word and still be complete sentence because the subject, though not written, is still understood. For example: *Stop!* The subject (you) is understood, so the one word forms a complete sentence.

Some people have a hard time identifying a complete sentence; therefore, they write sentence fragments, such as: *The president of our company. Down in the valley.* These sentences lack a subject, which, along with the verb, makes a complete idea: *John Smith (subject) is (verb) president of our company.*

The house (subject) is (verb) down in the valley.

When a sentence has a subject and a verb, it is called a *simple sentence*. A simple sentence may have some adjectives describing the noun and some adverbs describing the verb, but is it called a simple sentence because it expresses one complete idea with a subject and verb and no other additional thought.

A *compound sentence* contains two or more complete ideas usually joined together by a conjunction. There are seven conjunctions that are used to join compound sentences: *and, but, or, nor, for, so, yet.* An example of a compound sentence is the following:

The boy ran into the house, and the dog ran out the back door.

This sentence could be written without a conjunction. If the conjunction is dropped, a semicolon should be used; otherwise, you would have a run-on sentence. Here is how it could be written with a semicolon:

The boy ran into the house; the dog ran out the back door.

Note that each complete idea (called a clause) has a subject and verb and the two sentences (clauses) are joined by a conjunction with a comma. Except for very short compound sentences, a comma should always be put before the conjunction.

A *complex sentence* contains one main idea and at least one incomplete idea that will not stand by itself and make sense. Here is an example:

When you drive down the street, you will see all the beautiful trees and flowers.

The first idea in this sentence is not complete: *When you drive down the street.* The subject is *you* and the verb is *drive*, yet the idea is incomplete and will not make sense on its own. This is called a subordinate clause (a clause has a subject and verb and expresses a complete idea; subordinate clauses do not express complete ideas).

A fourth type of sentence is called a *compound-complex sentence*. This type of sentence has at least two complete ideas (main clauses) and at least one incomplete idea (subordinate clause). Here is an example of a compound-complex sentence:

> *If Fred is coming tomorrow, we need to clean the spare bedroom, and we need to buy more food.*

Once you are able to easily identify the basic types of sentence structures, you are well on your way to communicating with proper grammar.

Punctuating Sentences

The next important area for good grammar is punctuation. Punctuation makes it possible to read a sentence and get the complete idea. Here is an example:

> *What is is what is not is not is it not*

As written, these words make no sense at all, but with proper punctuation, the sentence is easily understood.

> *What is, is; what is not, is not; is it not?*

Another example is found in the story of a young man and woman who were sweethearts. After an argument one night, the young man wrote this note to the young woman:

> *Woman without her man is a beast.*

The young woman sent the note back to the young man. She added two marks of punctuation which changed the entire meaning of the sentence:

> *Woman! without her, man is a beast.*

These illustrations point out the importance of proper punctuation in order to communicate clearly. Let's look at the various marks of punctuation and discover their usage. Good writers do not necessarily know where marks of punctuation belong in sentences, rather they know how to use them properly. In this section you will learn how to use them properly.

The Comma

Let's tackle the toughest one first—the comma. The comma is used to help the reader move through words, phrases, and clauses that are not part of the main idea of the sentence. There are ten basic ways the comma is used in sentences:

1. Use the comma to separate a series of words in a sentence when connecting words (conjunctions) are not used.

    Example: The file contains red, blue, green, and yellow folders.

    Some grammarians claim the comma should not be used before the *and*, but it is a good idea to put one there so the last two ideas are not confused as one unit. If the comma is left out of the above sentence, one might conclude there are folders which are red, blue, green and yellow.

2. Use a comma in compound sentences to separate the main clauses. Remember, a compound sentence contains two main ideas (clauses) which could stand alone as separate sentences.

    Example: The stove was too hot, and we had to open some windows.

    If the compound sentence is short, a comma may not be necessary.

    Example: He came and I left.

3. Use a comma to separate a clause which does not make sense by itself from the rest of the sentence. This is sometimes called a *dependent clause* because it cannot stand alone as a sentence, but needs the rest of the sentence to complete the thought.

    Example: Waiting for the plane to arrive, we read several magazines.

4. Use a comma to separate nonessential words (sometimes called transition words) from the rest of the sentence.

Example: Therefore, we should seek his opinion first before preceding.

> Other introductory words are *yes, indeed, surely, however, furthermore, nevertheless, moreover, likewise, well, consequently,* etc.

5. Use a comma to separate nonessential information from the rest of the sentence.

Example: The third customer, who ordered the gloves, won the prize.

> Here is an example of nonessential information which actually depends on the intent of the writer. If the third customer is the one *who ordered the gloves,* then the information is essential. But if the third customer is one of three *who ordered the gloves,* then the information is nonessential; therefore, should be set off by commas.

6. Use a comma in direct address when you are writing to a person and using his/her name as if you were talking to the person.

Example: Joe, I really appreciate your help.

7. Use a comma to clarify confusion in a sentence.

Example: Since then, we have taken the long way home.

8. Use a comma to set off a direct quotation.

Example: John asked, "How are we to know if you don't tell us?"

9. Use a comma to set off a definite place, month, or year.

Example: New York, New York; January 1, 2000

10. Use a comma to set off an appositive (an appositive is a word or phrase that defines or identifies another word).

Example: Horace Duff, the new manager, is willing to listen to our complaints.

The Semicolon

The use of the semicolon was summarized very accurately by Nona Balakian:

> *"And what of the semicolon? Is it really to be scrapped? Not, surely, while there are writers around whose ideas follow a lateral pattern, who no sooner finish a thought than they feel another of equal weight emerging—all leading to a final note of elucidation."* —Nona Balakian in *The New York Times*, November 27, 1965

A semicolon is an upgraded comma indicating a longer pause than the comma, but not a complete stop or change of thought as with the period. Many people do not use the semicolon because they don't understand how to use it correctly. There are basically three ways to use the semicolon.

1. Use a semicolon to join two main thoughts (clauses) which could be separate, complete sentences.

   Example: The big hand on the clock is pointing to four; the little hand on the clock is pointing to twelve.

2. Use a semicolon to separate items in a series when the items contain commas.

   Example: The people attending the meeting are Joe Guinn, president; Elaine Moyers, vice president; Glenn Ford, treasurer; and Rita Ellis, secretary.

3. Use a semicolon with conjunctive adverbs (e.g., however, therefore, moreover, etc.) which introduce a second main clause.

   Example: She has an excellent background in computer graphics; however, she is weak in sales experience.

The Colon

The colon is used to introduce important material or a significant theme. It is like the blare of trumpets before the grand entrance. There are three ways to use the colon correctly.

1. The colon is used to introduce lists, examples, etc. The colon means *as follows.*

Example: The following information is needed: age, driver's license, occupation, and place of employment. *Note:* Do not use a colon after the word *are*, which introduces a list that is the object of the sentence.

Example: The things needed to complete the information are age, driver's license, occupation, and place of employment.

2. The colon is used to introduce a single word or phrase in order to give dramatic impact.

Example: There is one thing we all need to succeed: enthusiasm.

If the colon introduces a complete sentence, capitalize the first letter of the word which follows the colon (There is one thing to remember: Always listen before speaking.)

3. The colon is used after the salutation in a business letter (Dear Mr. Jones:), and to write time (7:00 a.m.), and to separate chapter and verse in Bible citations (John 3:16).

Because of the confusion that exists in the use of the semicolon, colon, and period, here is a helpful guideline:

- Use a period to close one thought before beginning another.
- Use a semicolon to give equal balance to two main thoughts in a sentence.
- Use a colon to emphasize the second thought in a sentence more than the first thought.

The Period

The period ends a complete thought; it is a full stop at the end of the sentence.

Example: The boy ran home.

The period is also used after abbreviations and initials.

Example: Mrs. Ms. Mr. J. P. Smith

The Ellipsis

An ellipsis (three dots) is a way of saying, "I have omitted some words from the original." It can also mean a lapse of time or something has been left to the reader's imagination. If the incomplete statement comes at the beginning or in the middle of a sentence, three dots are used. If the ellipsis comes at the beginning of a statement, the first word does not need to be capitalized. If it comes at the end of one of your sentences, four dots are used—three dots for the incomplete statement and one for the period.

Examples:

". . . ask what you can do for your country."

Mother said, "If only you could understand . . . ."

The Hyphen

The hyphen tells the reader two or more words are being joined together. They are to be understood as a unit, and they describe a noun (i.e., adjectives).

Examples: an extra-base hit; all-night debate; seven-year-old son; hard-to-please audience; first-class seat.

There is much disagreement concerning when to hyphenate certain words. Here is a list of prefixes that are usually hyphenated; however, it is suggested that an up-to-date style guide be used as a reference because opinions are constantly changing concerning these and other prefixes.

self: When this word is used as a prefix, it is always hyphenated. *self-conscious, self-defeating, self-centered, etc.*

half: Sometimes this prefix is not hyphenated (e.g., *halfhearted, halfback*), other times, it is hyphenated (*half-truth, half-dollar, etc.*).

ex: This prefix is hyphenated, usually, when followed by a noun (*ex-officer, ex-champion, ex-marine*).

co: Like the prefix *ex, co* is hyphenated before nouns (*co-pilot, co-worker, co-star*).

anti: Most of the time, this prefix becomes part of the word, except when the letter *i* follows (anti-intellectual).

re: This prefix is sometimes hyphenated to prevent confusion (*re-form*, to form again; *re-cover;* to cover again, but "to recover from the mistake" is not hyphenated; *re-collect*, to collect again, but "to recollect the mistake" is not hyphenated. The same applies to: re-collect; re-lease; re-marked; re-press; re-sort; re-sign; re-treat, etc.).

In addition to the above, a hyphen is often used in spelling prefixes that end with the same letter as the beginning of the word (*re-established, re-engineer, pre-entry, etc.*).

The hyphen is also used for spelling numbers between 20 and 200 (*twenty-five, thirty-eight, etc.*). The same applies to spelling fractions (*three-fifths, seven-eights, etc.*).

The Parentheses

Parentheses are used to set off words, phrases, clauses, or complete sentences. They are used to tell the reader that the additional information is an *aside* ("by the way" kind of information). The additional information may be explanations or clarifications or maybe definitions of unfamiliar words. Parentheses are also used with numbers to provide dates or to give emphasis to a number.

Examples:

She has Tetanus (lockjaw).

The car came out of nowhere (I couldn't believe how fast!) and hit my car broadside.

There are twenty (20) people on one bus.

The information is in chapter ten (p. 20).

The Dash

Dashes (more properly called *em dashes*) are often used to show strong feelings, opinions, thoughts, or to insert a sudden change of subject.

Example: The teacher—if only she knew the truth!—thinks she is liked by everyone.

It is not necessary to punctuate the statement that is set off by the dash unless there is a need to place strong emphasis or if it is a question. The dash is usually not found on a keyboard, but may be located in *symbol* inside *Insert* if you are using Microsoft Word. If you don't want to go to the trouble finding the dash there, just hit the hyphen twice. Do not space before, in between, or after the two hyphens (--).

The Brackets

Brackets are usually used inside quotation marks to indicate that the words are not part of the original quotation. They usually give additional information or may reflect the opinion of the writer.

Examples: "He [Charles Hightower] is captain of the football team."

You may see the Latin word *sic* in brackets [*sic*]. When it is inside a quotation, it means: "This is the way it appeared in the original. Don't blame me for the misspelling or misuse. I know better."

You may find it necessary to put parentheses inside parentheses, when that's the case, it's better to use brackets for the inner parentheses.

The Quotation Marks

Quotation marks are used to tell the reader: These are the *exact* words of the person who said them. It is important to remember that the period is always placed inside quotation marks at the end of the sentence before the last set of quotations marks.

Example: Mrs. Hampton said, "All students must practice their music daily."

Question marks and exclamation points are placed either inside or outside quotation marks depending on whether they belong to the quoted statement or the entire sentence.

Examples:

Fred asked, "Is it going to rain?"

Who said, "Give me liberty or give me death"?

In the first example, if the sentence is reworded into a question, it would be punctuated the same: *Was it Fred who asked, "Is it going to rain?"* You would not use two quotation marks in such a case.

Don't use quotation marks if you are paraphrasing another person's statement. To paraphrase means to put the statement in your own words, or maybe to shorten it by omitting some words.

Example: The coach said we should try harder to win.

If quotation marks are used for a quotation that includes more than one paragraph, quotations are used at the beginning of each paragraph but are only placed at the end of the last paragraph.

Quotation marks are placed around titles of songs, short stories, short poems, essays, articles, and chapter titles which appear within larger works. The titles of books, magazines, newspapers, movies, operas, and full-length plays are either underlined or put in italics. Single quotation marks are used to set off a quotation within a quotation.

The Question Mark

The question mark is used after a *direct* question but not after an *indirect* question. An *indirect* question is one for which an answer is not expected.

Examples:

The only question is how to get it there. (indirect question)

Do you know how we are going to get it there? (direct question)

The Exclamation Mark

The exclamation mark is at the end of sentences which express surprise, emotion, or deep feeling.

Example: Watch out for that tree!

The exclamation mark is also used after an interjection (Wow! Oh!) or a word used as an interjection (Hurry!).

The exclamation mark can also be used at the end of a sentence that sounds like a question but has strong feeling or emotion.

Example: How could she do that!

The Apostrophe

The Apostrophe is used to show possession. Here is a simple guideline to remember in order to use the apostrophe correctly: If the singular form of the noun does not end in **s** or an **s** sound, add the apostrophe and **s** ('s).

Singular	*Singular Possessive*
boy	boy's
girl	girl's
lady	lady's

If the noun ends in **s** or an **s** sound, add the apostrophe after the **s**. Some nouns can take an additional **s** after the apostrophe if the **s** is sounded (e.g., boss's, dress's, etc.)

Noun	*Possessive*
boys	boys'
girls	girls'
ladies	ladies'
boss	boss' or boss's

dress	dress' or dress's
box	box' or box's

Plural nouns form possessive by simply adding apostrophe and **s**.

Plural	*Plural Possessive*
men	men's
children	children's
teeth	teeth's
geese	geese's

The singular and plural possessives of compound nouns are formed by adding the apostrophe to the end of the compound word.

Singular	*Plural*
brother-in-law's	brothers-in-law's
mother-in-law's	mothers-in-law's

The apostrophe is also used in forming contractions.

Examples: don't, hadn't, wouldn't, it's

Common Errors

Once you have a good working knowledge of the parts of speech, the various kinds of sentences, and the marks of punctuation, the foundation has been laid for a proper use of grammar. The remainder of this chapter will deal with some of the most common mistakes made by writers and speakers.

Double Negatives

A double negative is a sentence that contains more than one negative within the same clause. (Negatives: no, not, nor, neither, none, never, no, one, hardly, scarcely)

Incorrect: He *never* has *no* money.

Correct: He *never* has any money. or He has *no* money.

The Problem with I and Me

You should begin sentences with *I*, which is always the subject of the sentence. Use *me* when it's used as an object of verbs or prepositions.

Incorrect: Bob and me went to the movie.

Correct: Bob and I went to the movie.

Incorrect: The bus picked up John and I.

Correct: The bus picked up John and me.

Other personal pronouns work the same as *I*. Be sure to use *he, she, we, they* as subjects, and *him, her, us, them* as objects of verbs and prepositions.

The Problem of Like and As

You should use *like* before nouns, pronouns, and gerunds and *as* should be used before phrases and clauses.

Incorrect: She looks like she is angry.

Correct: She looks as if she is angry. (*She is angry* is a clause.)

Correct: She looks like her sister.

The Problem of Pronouns not Agreeing with Their Antecedents

The rule is that pronouns must agree in number, case, and gender with their antecedents (the word they rename).

Incorrect: The board announced their plans.

Correct: The board announced its plans.

Incorrect: Everyone should pick up their coat.

Correct: Everyone should pick up his/her coat. (note: In order to use gender-free language, you can write it as in the example, or you could write: All should pick up their coats.)

Incorrect: The man who shouted was him.

Correct: The man who shouted was he. (When a pronoun follows a form of the verb to be (am, are, is, was, were), it must be in the nominative, not objective, case. You can double-check yourself by turning the sentence around: He was the man who shouted.

The Problem of Double Comparisons

You should not use *more* or *most* when *-er* or *-est* is added to a modifier.

Incorrect: The bus is *more roomier* since the seats were taken out.

Correct: The bus is *roomier* since the seats were taken out.

The Problem of Unnecessary Prepositions

You should omit prepositions that add nothing to the meaning of the sentence.

Incorrect: Where is the ball at?

Correct: Where is the ball?

Incorrect: He jumped off of the cliff.

Correct: He jumped off the cliff.

Incorrect: They walked outside of the building.

Correct: They walked outside the building.

The Problem of Unparalleled Sentences

Parallelism means all items in a sentence should be structured equally.

Incorrect: He works in the garden, mows the lawn, and relaxed afterward.

Correct: He works in the garden, mows the lawn, and relaxes afterward.

The Problem with And and Try

This is a mistake you will see often. The verb *try* should be followed by *to*, not *and*.

Incorrect: Would you try and answer the question correctly?

Correct: Would you try to answer the question correctly?

The Problem with Could Of and Could Have

The contraction of *could have* is *could've*. When pronounced, it sounds like *could of*, which is why this mistake is often made.

Incorrect: I could of spent the day at the park.

Correct: I could have spent the day at the park.

The Problem with Different Than

It is incorrect to write or say *different than*. It should always be *different from*.

Incorrect: I am different than you in that respect.

Correct: I am different from you in that respect.

Capitalization

One more area of importance in order to round out a proper use of grammar for effective communication is capitalization. Here are some good guidelines for using capital letters:

- Proper nouns (people, places, races, languages, days of the week, months, special days, historical periods and events, trade names, deity, companies).
- Positions or job titles (Capitalize these only when preceding a name. If they follow a name, do not capitalize. I saw Mayor Jane Smith today. I saw Jane Smith, mayor, today.).
- First letter of sentences.
- First word of a direct quotation.
- The first word and all principal words in headings and titles (as well as prepositions of four letters or more).
- The first word of each line of poetry.
- The first and principal words in addresses.
- The first words in salutations and closings.

There it is! Master this chapter and you will be well on your way to communicating effectively with proper grammar.

Chapter 6

How to Communicate with Proper Etiquette

You have no doubt heard that one does not get a second chance to make a first impression, or it takes only ten or fifteen seconds to make a first impression—and the rest of your life to undo it if it's a negative one. Both of these statements contain some elements of truth. People generally form their impressions of you during the first few seconds of initial contact. They observe your clothes, hair, facial expressions, body language, eye contact, gestures, and voice as well as the words you actually speak. Taken together, these form an impression in the mind of the observer about the person you are, whether you can be trusted, if you care about him/her, and if you are an interesting person.

There are some things you can do to create a positive impression as people get to know you better. These things are called "etiquette," or a better word is simply: manners. They contribute to your ability to communicate well with others and, in many cases, to get along with others. John D. Rockefeller once said, "The ability to get along with people is as purchasable a commodity as sugar and coffee, and I pay more for that ability than any under the sun."

Today we live in a high-tech/high-touch business environment. Most people are hired for their ability to perform a job (high-tech), but they keep that job because they have the ability to get along with others (high-touch). In our global community, the knowledge of what is appropriate and what is not can go a long way in helping a person maintain good relationships and, consequently, keep a job.

There is perhaps nothing that can contribute to an employee's or executive's ability to create a successful image more than the ability to handle others with tact and style. We often call these abilities "social skills." They are absolutely necessary when it comes to building good relationships with others. In this book I have already given some helpful guidelines on how to relate positively to others. A very important part of relating to others is having the knowledge of what things constitute good manners. This chapter will cover those. There are six contemporary needs which are often neglected in teaching proper manners: table and eating manners, proper introductions, global respect, workplace diversity, job interviews, and travel

Table and Eating Manners

It would be helpful to know the various items you will encounter at your table. So beginning on the left of your plate will be the *seafood fork*. It is used for shrimp, clams, oysters, snails, and other types of seafood which may be served as a first course. If this is not on the left by the first fork, then it will be on the right beside the knives and soup spoon. Next is the *fish fork*. It is sometimes interchangeable with the salad fork. A true fish fork has one specially shaped tine used to pull apart the fish. Next is the *place fork* used for the main meal. Then the *salad fork*, which may be on the left of the *place fork* if the salad is served before the main course. If the salad is after the main course, the *salad fork* will be on the right of the *place fork*.

Moving to the right of your plate, there will be a *soup spoon/fruit spoon*. Only, of course, if soup or fruit is being served. Next is the *fish knife*, provided fish is being served, if not, the next item will be the *dinner knife,* which is used for the main course. Then you may find a *dessert/coffee spoon*, which is sometimes above the plate or on the right of the plate. Next will be the *dessert fork*. On the top of the bread plate will be the *butter knife*.

There are usually three plates at a setting. The *bread plate* is placed slightly to the left and above the dinner plate. The *salad plate* or bowl will be on the left of the dinner plate. Sometimes there will be a small plate on top of the dinner plate which will be used for seafood or an appetizer.

If you are attending a very formal dinner, there may be a finger bowl above and to the left of the dinner plate. It is not used until dessert is finished. Although at Chinese or Japanese dinners it will be brought out before the meal. Whether it is brought out before or after the meal, you use it the same way. You dip your fingers into the water and remove them and dry them with your napkin. On certain occasions, and especially in First Class on some airlines, you will receive a hot towel. It is not proper to use it to wipe your face, only your hands.

Here are some suggestions concerning how to eat certain foods:

Soup: Most etiquette books suggest dipping the spoon into the soup and moving it away from the body. It is proper to tip the bowl slightly to get the last spoonful, but it is not a good idea to lift the bowl and drink directly from it.

Salad: If the salad fork will not cut the salad, a knife may be used. When you are finished with the soup and salad, leave the utensils in or on the side of the bowl and on the salad plate.

Main Course: There are two acceptable styles of eating a main course meal. The American Method is the most common. The knife is held in the right hand and the fork is held in the left with the tines down holding the meat or whatever item is being cut. After a bite has been cut, the knife is laid down at the top of the plate with serrated edge facing you, and the fork is transferred to the right hand with the tines facing up, and the food is carried to the mouth. The Continental Method (sometime called European Method) is the same as the American Method until the food has been cut. Then the knife is held in the right hand while the left hand brings the food to the mouth with the fork (tines are kept down). The proper way to hold the knife in the right hand while cutting is to keep the index finger on the handle slightly overlapping the blade. The fork should be held in the left hand with the index finger extending down on the back of the fork. The elbows should be slightly above the table level.

If you should need to lay the fork and knife down while eating, place the knife at the top of your plate with serrated edge facing you. Place the fork, tines up, on your place with the handle resting on the lower right side of the plate. The Continental Method of resting involves placing the knife on the plate first, with its handle to the lower right of the plate, and the fork, tines down, is placed on the lower left of the plate so the fork and knife cross.

When you have finished eating, place your fork across the center of the plate with the handle to the right and the tines down. Place the knife next to the fork with the blade still facing you. In the Continental Method, place both utensils in the center of your plate with the handles toward you and the ends of both utensils at a 12 o'clock position on your plate.

It doesn't matter which style (American or Continental) you use. But it is important in very formal settings to be consistent in the method used and not swap back and forth.

Bread: If a roll or slice of bread is served, tear off a bite-sized piece, butter it, then lay the butter knife across the top of your bread plate, serrated edge toward you. After eating the first piece, proceed with the above guideline for the second, etc. A person without class will cut the roll in half, butter both halves, and begin eating. Following the proper technique will communicate a style of elegance that some will definitely notice! Also, it is proper to use the bread to get a small or difficult bit of food, but it is not considered acceptable to use bread to wipe your plate clean, no matter how good the food may have been or how much you want to show your host you enjoyed the meal.

Spaghetti: The proper way to eat spaghetti is to use a fork to twirl it and a spoon to assist in securing the strands to the fork. This is doing it truly Italian!

Corn on the cob: Think of eating like a typewriter types, going across the entire cob, a few rows at a time, either left to right or right to left.

Chicken: In a formal setting, chicken should not be eaten with the fingers, no matter how finger lickin' good it may be! Use a knife and fork.

Ribs: There is probably only one way to eat ribs: with the fingers. But if you are in a very formal setting, which would probably never serve ribs, you never go wrong using the knife and fork.

Seafood: Use the small fork and knife and eat from the seafood plate. You may use your fingers to eat shrimp. If they are large, eat them in two bites instead on one big bite. Place the tails on the seafood plate. Oysters, and clams are usually served in ice. A seafood fork should be used. While holding the shell in place with one hand, use the seafood fork to lift the oyster or clam out of the shell and eat it in one bite. The shell should not be picked up. If sauce is served, dip each piece in the sauce before eating. If steamed clams are served, use your fingers to lift each clam by its neck, then pull the body from the neck and discard the neck. Dip the clam in melted butter or broth and eat in one bite. Lobsters are eaten with a tool that looks like a nutcracker. Use it to crack open the two big claws, then break them apart with your hands. Use the seafood fork to dig out the meat holding the claw in your left hand. After the meat is on your plate, it can be eaten a bite at a time, dipping each bite in the butter sauce.

One important area often overlooked is the use of the napkin. Here are some pointers:

1. Be sure to wait for the host to put a napkin in his or her lap before you do. If there is no host, wait until everyone has been seated.
2. If the napkin is in a goblet, it is proper to wait for the server to unfold it and place it in your lap.
3. If you place your own napkin, don't shake it out; rather, open it and place it in your lap, but be sure it is folded in half with the crease toward you.
4. Use the napkin to remove food from your lips before you drink a beverage.
5. At the close of the meal, keep your napkin on your lap until everyone has finished eating and drinking. Then place the napkin on the right side of your plate.

Proper Introductions

Introductions are based on hierarchy. The person being introduced is named last. Speak to the greater authority first: "Mr./Ms. CEO, I'd like to introduce Mr./Ms. Junior Executive." Here are some examples of order for introductions:

1. Younger to older.
2. Junior to senior.
3. Gender?—either! (The old rule of etiquette stated the female was named first, today that distinction is no longer in vogue).
4. Untitled to titled.

When introducing a woman by her last name, it is preferred by most women to be introduced as "Ms." Ministers, rabbis, priests, and other clergy along with judges are introduced by using their titles.

If you're introducing two people who live together or two partners, it is not necessary to make reference to their relationship. Simply give their names; further conversation can reveal their relationship as they choose to give such information. After making an introduction, it is appropriate to explain the relationship each person has with you. For example: " Joe Jones, this is Fred Friendly. Fred is a college roommate of mine. Mr. Jones is president and CEO of our company."

Global Respect

Every culture has its own particular quirks and idiosyncrasies. There is, however, one universal language that the entire world recognizes: the smile. It is a form of international communications that shows friendliness and openness. Beyond that, every culture is different from all others. There are some parts of the world where the woman is still treated with old-fashioned manners: standing when she enters the room, opening the door for the her, carrying her briefcase, etc. In a Muslim country, it is considered a grave social offense to shake hands with a woman. In other cultures, these traditions have been abandoned and the woman is given egalitarian treatment.

It is wise, if you are traveling to another country, to research their culture to determine the dos and don'ts of that culture. Some books are listed in the bibliography that can be of some assistance.

In some cultures, the handshake, for example, is a positive form of greeting; others greet with bows, applause, and prayerful hands. Looking someone in the eye gives offense in some countries; others (e.g., the USA) perceive the lack of eye contact as shady or dishonest.

The Japanese love giving gifts. When a citizen of Japan travels abroad, the citizen takes along *o-tsukai mono* or small "things to be used." These are gifts, usually fans, scarves, or some small electronic gadgets, which are given to others who may assist the citizen of Japan in some way. Therefore, if you are traveling in Japan, it would be a good idea to take along some "things to be used" as gifts.

It is important to be aware of gift-giving customs in various countries as well as in various companies. In China, if a clock is given as a gift it is considered bad luck. In some companies, gift giving is taboo because the gift may be perceived as a bribe or a favor. If, however, it is appropriate to give gifts in your business culture, here are some areas that gifts would be appropriate:

- When a project is completed
- Holidays (including ALL religious holidays)
- When a person is promoted
- To celebrate: a wedding, birth of a child, a move, retirement, a business milestone, a new job, etc
- When you offend someone or missed an appointment
- When someone has gone to great lengths to help you on a project
- Use your own creative ideas

Here is a list of suggested ideas for appropriate gifts:

- Food (ham, turkey, ostrich, etc.)
- Flowers (usually can be used cross-culturally in some cases)
- Tickets (to theater, opera, sports events)
- Cakes (for birthday, anniversaries)
- Wine (Be aware that this is considered inappropriate in some cases, so know your recipients well enough to not offend.)

Diversity in the Workplace

Companies today have a broad background of cultures and viewpoints in the same workplace. These cultures and viewpoints create communication and leadership challenges for supervisors and managers. The term that identifies these challenges is *workplace diversity*. Today's leaders must learn how to communicate with empathy and understanding to a diverse work force.

The first prerequisite is self-awareness. Leaders must have an understanding of their own socialization, that is, what things have influenced them in their own culture, what is considered good etiquette, and what constitutes poor manners. Without this knowledge, the leader can become unwittingly biased toward other cultures.

After self-awareness, the next step is to become knowledgeable about the diverse backgrounds of the people who work for their organization. Simple areas of etiquette, such as awareness of gender-biased speech, can make a world of difference in how well a leader communicates with his/her people. Leaders (executives, CEOs, managers, supervisors, presidents) must create workplace environments that nurture the benefits of diversity and resolve the challenges.

One important area of workplace diversity that poses a challenge to many leaders is communicating with people who have disabilities. Here are some important guidelines to keep in mind that will provide proper manners toward the mobility impaired:

- Offer help only if it appears help is needed—don't insist.
- Don't hover over the person.
- If a person with disability falls, don't rush immediately to his/her aid. The person may want to get up alone.
- Don't remove crutches or wheelchairs away unless the person wants them taken out of the way.
- Let the person tell you how to help. Don't just step in without a request for help.
- Always ask the person if you can give assistance, even if it is marginal assistance. For example, opening the door too wide for a person on crutches may cause the person to fall if the door is used as a support.

Job Interview

The first step in etiquette for a job interview is called: research. Finding out as much information as possible on the company you're interviewing with is absolutely necessary in order to perform well in the interview. Here are some areas to research:

- History
- Profit/loss profile
- Public image
- Future plans
- Any problems

A word of caution, however. This information should come only from public records, etc. Any internal information from employees could be politically influenced and, therefore, inaccurate.

Always dress properly for a job interview. What is proper differs with each company and from city to city. A good general rule is that one should dress as if going to work the first day with the company in the position one is seeking. Again, research will give you the answer to the question: What should I wear? All professions have unwritten dress codes, as do all companies. The guiding principle is always *conservative*.

The whole ritual of job interviewing is designed to show that you understand the etiquette of your particular career field. So here are some guidelines that will help you conduct a solid job interview:

1. Create a positive image with *everyone* you meet (receptionist, secretary, etc.) The person who conducts the interview may ask their opinion of you.
2. Watch your watch! Be on time! One of the strongest negative messages you can send a potential employer is to be late for the interview.
3. Offer to shake hands first. Old etiquette books suggested the prospective employee should wait for the interviewer to offer to shake hands. Today those old rules are no longer followed regardless of the gender. So be assertive and extend your hand first.
4. Watch your manners. Don't chew gum or smoke or eat candy before or during the interview.
5. It is advisable not to call the interviewer by his or her first name unless the interviewer indicates a preference. Don't ask the interviewer for a preference, wait until you are instructed. If there is no indication the interviewer wants to be called by his or her first name, then use only the last name. If the interviewer is a woman, call her "Ms." You are always safe with this title.
6. Watch your body language. When seated, don't fidget; instead, sit up straight but not stiff, and make good eye contact with the interviewer. Keep your body posture open—don't fold your arms across the front of your body. Review the chapter on body language before your interview so these pointers will be fresh in your mind.
7. Be a good listener. Wait until the interviewer has finished the question/statement before responding. A good suggestion is to count to three (or even five!) after the last statement before responding. That assures you the interviewer has finished the statement. Otherwise, you may find yourself in the embarrassing position of having

interrupted the interviewer before he or she has finished talking.

8. Demonstrate self-assurance. Remember that the interviewer is trying to determine one thing: How much will you benefit his or her company? Your confident answers can assure the interviewer that you are the right person for the job. Be careful not to appear too cocky, which is a turn-off for most interviewers.

9. Stay alert to the interviewer's tactics. Many times interviewers will use tactics to get you to open up and divulge things that will give them more information about you. Sometimes interviewers will take you into their confidence in order to get you to confess things you would normally not reveal about yourself. It is hoped you would not have anything to hide, but sometimes it is best not to reveal everything about yourself, especially if you have a black mark somewhere in your past. Sometimes interviewers will use rudeness to test you. Your response will tell them how you react under pressure.

10. Answer open-ended questions with care. Open-ended questions have two purposes when used by skilled interviewers. One purpose is to put you at ease. Another reason is to encourage you to ramble on and on about one particular question that will reveal more about you.

11. Don't lie. This should go without saying, but sometimes you may be tempted to exaggerate a particular accomplishment or misrepresent the reason you were laid off. Such false information will come back to haunt you later, maybe resulting in your losing a good job opportunity that otherwise would have been yours had you been truthful. Some potential areas that tempt some to lie are past salaries, problem areas with other employers, and past accomplishments. Honesty is the best policy in all of these areas.

12. Be careful with humor. Some job interviews have turned into sessions that were full of laughs, but with no real substance. The interviewer was able to lead the

prospective employee into revealing a flippant side that cost him or her the job. If the interviewer tells a joke, laugh; however, don't respond with another joke. Interviews that turn into joke sessions rarely result in employment.

13. Don't overextend your welcome. Watch for signals the interviewer is drawing the interview to an end. Statements such as "It has been a pleasure meeting you" or "Thank you for your time" are indications the interviewer wants to end the discussion. Even though you may have some additional things to say, it would be best to save them for a letter which you can write later.

14. End the interview with a positive statement about how much you would enjoy working with the company. Be sure to give a good, solid reason for wanting to work for the company, rather than a general statement about your need for employment or desire for career advancement with the new company.

15. Follow up the interview with a brief "thank you" note to the interviewer. If it is on personal stationary, that will create a more professional image for you in the mind of the interviewer. Be sure to identify one aspect of the interview you enjoyed. Tie it to some aspect of the company's operation to indicate you would be a team player. Example: "I was very impressed with the ways ABC Company strives for customer satisfaction. That is the kind of professional environment I would find challenging and rewarding."

Travel

Most of us recognize the need for good etiquette in relation to those we contact day after day. One area often overlooked is etiquette in travel. A large part of my job involves travel, so here are some things I've learned which should be helpful:

Air Travel

If you have to move about on an airplane after takeoff, it would be a good idea to request an aisle seat when making your reservations.

Be careful about striking up a conversation with your fellow passenger. Some people do not like to talk to others while on an airline. Watch their body language, notice their eye contact (or lack of it); if the signs are positive, you can test them to see if they want to talk. If their response is short and they continue to read the book or look through the magazine, it would be advisable to discontinue any further efforts to communicate.

Also, show respect to the flight attendants. Their jobs are stressful at times, and they may not have time for your insignificant requests. You should not push the call bell unless there is an emergency. If you do have a request, word it in such a way that it doesn't sound pressing: "If you have time, please . . . . " When you deboard, be sure to thank them for their service. Remember, their main responsibility is your safety, not to be your servant.

When deboarding, be sure to wait until everyone in the seats in front of you has started out the aisle. It is an unwritten rule in airline travel to not cut in front of the persons seated in front of you when deboarding. The only exception to this is if your arrival time has caused you to have close connections with your next flight. In that case, you should inform the attendant that you need to deboard as quickly as possible to make your connection. In most cases, the attendant will assist you in deboarding in front of those who do not have close connections.

Taxi

In most countries, except Australia, passengers ride in the back seat of the cab. In Australia, if you are the only person traveling, it is appropriate, and even expected, that you will ride in the front. When traveling with business associates, junior executives should choose to sit in the front seat of the cab and offer the back seat to the senior executives. It is also proper for the junior executive to offer to pay the fare and tip. If the senior executives insist on paying, the junior executive should not insist any further.

Automobile

One issue that is confusing today is: Should one open the door for a male or female traveling companion? If the door is locked, it is good manners to unlock the door and open it. The passenger can take it from there.

When driving, it is bad manners to turn the radio or stereo up loud enough to drown out any possible conversation. You should ask your passenger what type of music he or she likes and then try to accommodate if the trip is going to take several hours.

Courtesy behind the wheel has become a real issue in many large cities today. Such things as driving too slowly in the passing lane, cutting in front of others, and tailgating are still considered bad driving manners. Of course, any negative body language (such as the ancient Roman gesture *digitus impudicus*, or impudent finger, the extended middle digit!) is considered out of place and rude. It should go without saying that aggressive driving (sometimes called road rage) is out of place and very dangerous. Of the 41,907 highway fatalities in 1996, one-third of these crashes and about two-thirds of the resulting fatalities can be attributed to behavior associated with aggressive driving. Aggressive driving is characterized by such things as: speeding, failing to yield, weaving in and out of traffic, passing on the right side, making improper lane changes, running stop signs and lights, screaming, honking, and flashing the lights. Driving with consideration is not only the right thing to do, it can also save lives!

Little Things Count

Many rules of etiquette have gone through paradigm shifts in today's business world. It is important to stay current on these changes. Little things can add up, and the image you communicate should always be one of a polished professional. The guidelines in this chapter form a solid base to help you project the kind of image that will be admired and respected by your peers.

Chapter 7

How to Communicate with Effective Leadership

Here is the biggest understatement you will read for the next ten years: We are living in a time of constant change! You would have to be living on an island in the middle of the ocean, completely cut off from all contact with the known world, not to realize the truthfulness of that statement.

Here is a brief history of time: hunter/gatherer society (perhaps 10 million years), planter/gardener or agrarian society (8,000 years), urban industrial society (200 years), global communication society (25 years). The changes from the hunter/gatherer society to an agricultural society were obviously very slow. The transition from an agricultural society to an industrial society was much faster. But the change from the industrial society to our present-day global communication society has been incredibly rapid.

The quantum leap in our gobal communication society's technology has produced for the average person a lifestyle of constant change. Computer technology alone has changed most people's lives. Our seven-year-old grandson knows how to "surf the net," send e-mail, and play complex computer games. I cannot imagine what incredible changes he will live to see in computer technology in the next 30-50 years.

We now hear about smart offices, smart homes, smart cars, smart telephones, all of which will respond to our needs with a simple voice command or voiceprint, as it is called. You can no longer go to a library and find a book in the card files, you must know how to use the computer. In addition, we have voice mail, electronic mail, automatic pay-at-the-pump gasoline stations, automatic cash machines (ATMs), and the list continues to grow. Some banks have begun charging an extra fee if you want to speak to a "live" teller instead of using the automation.

The developments in medical technology are mindboggling. Some day there will be eyeglasses available to create almost perfect night vision as well as day vision. Prosthesis will soon replace any part of the body except perhaps the brain. The subject of genetic engineering and cloning are topics that are almost too fearful to think about. Most of us would be surprised to know the advances we've made and the capabilities we have today in these areas.

A car was recently tested in California that is capable of doing its own steering and braking. It responds to sensors in the pavement and on the side of the highway as well as sensors in the front of the car that warn when it nears an object. Before long our cars will be able to drive themselves while we send our faxes, read our e-mails, check the internet, conduct conference calls, and enjoy a second cup of coffee from the coffee maker . . . all from the comfort of the automobile!

Jennifer James, in her book *Thinking in the Future Tense,* writes about a "sidebrain":

> *Already, surgeons wear headsets that retrieve information from their clinical data bank during operations. Rescue for the rest of us is on the way. I call it a "sidebrain," and somebody is making one right now. A big step past the Newton, Marco, or Envoy, it will clip on your belt like a pager and be voiced activated. It will answer your questions about spelling, math, scheduling, navigation, and other data. It will have a recognition beam, so that when someone is walking toward you, you can ask, "Do I know that person?" It will answer, in a whisper, "Yes, you do," and quickly tell you who that person is."*

As I list some of these changes, I find myself hesitating to even mention them for fear they will be obsolete by the time this book is published!

I recently talked to a man attending one of my public seminars whose great grandfather was a Native American who fought with Sitting Bull at the Battle of Littlebig Horn (1876) when General George Custer was defeated, and actually witnessed the death of General Custer. This Native American lived to be 105 years old. Just think of that! He lived from the days of Custer to the days of jet planes, computers, television, and the automobile. He actually witnessed the landing on the moon!

As dramatic as that seems, many of you reading this book have experienced incredible developments and changes in your lives as well. The learning curve for all of us is moving in a vertical direction. With the increase in technology, many changes are taking place in the workplace. Perhaps no change is as dramatic as that of the type of leaders and managers emerging in today's business world.

The new leader emerging today must have skills in two important areas: an understanding of self (called emotional intelligence) and an understanding of people (often called "people skills").

Emotional Intelligence

Emotional quotient, or EQ, is a measure of one's ability to identify and use emotions effectively. Research is bearing out the fact that emotional quotient or intelligence contributes more to one's success in the business world than any other quality. Some companies are requiring prospective employees to take EQ tests before employment. Psychologists agree that IQ (intelligence quotient) contributes to about 20 percent of a person's success, but EQ contributes a full 80 percent of a person's success. There are now more than 700 school districts in the United States considering programs that will help students raise their EQ.

The whole idea of emotional intelligence was originated by Dr. Peter Salovey of Yale University. It was popularized by Dr. Daniel Goleman in his best-selling book *Emotional Intelligence* (see bibliography for info). People who are considered leaders have the ability to tap into their own emotions and use them effectively in communicating passion or commitment or frustration, depending on what emotion is felt and needed at any particular moment. In addition, outstanding leaders have learned how to *listen* to the emotions of others and know what is happening inside or emotionally with a person at any given moment.

Dr. Goleman identified several major qualities that make up emotional intelligence. Each will be listed below with some suggestions on how they can be developed more fully.

1. Self-awareness. This is the ability to recognize a feeling the moment it happens. This means you are so in touch with your own emotional life that when a particular feeling comes to you, such as anger, fear, depression, you are able to immediately identify it as such.

Antonio Damasio, in his book *Descartes Error*, stated that a person who has developed a keen sense of his/her own self-awareness has what Damasio called "somatic markers" or, literally, gut feelings. Gut feelings can exist without one being aware of them. For example, when a person fears snakes subconsciously and is shown a picture of a snake, sensors on his/her skin will detect sweat, even if the person does not "feel" fear at that moment, realizing it is only a picture. The sweat is a sign of anxiety.

But a person with a high degree of self-awareness is tuned in to his/her gut feelings at that particular moment. The ability to develop this self-awareness is something all of us possess. With deliberate effort, it is possible to for us to become more aware of our feelings at any given moment.

Another example of this might be the person who is angered by a rude or offensive remark. The feeling of anger may linger for hours without the person's awareness, and without realizing it, the person might expose that anger toward someone else who has no knowledge nor awareness of the offense. By evaluating the feelings and identifying the anger, the angry person can change the feeling and shake off the bad mood.

2. Mood Management. The ability to stay in touch with one's emotions at any given point in time helps that person to develop mood management. We have little control over the things that happen to us that affect us emotionally. But we have some say in *how* we respond to what happens to us emotionally.

A once popular theory of psychology was ventilating will make one feel better. But after some research into this theory, it was discovered that outbursts of rage actually increase the brain's arousal system, and the person becomes more angry instead of less.

A better technique is what is called "reframing." This technique involves a conscious reinterpretation of an event or situation into a more positive light. For example, if a car cuts you off on the freeway, and you have not developed self-awareness, you might angrily shout, "*You idiot! You could have caused a wreck!*" Reframing the situation might involve saying to yourself, "*Perhaps he has an emergency.*" or "*I am not going to allow that person to ruin my day with his/her driving.*"

Another way to defuse anger is to find a place to cool down and think through the situation. Deep breathing and meditation are also good techniques in addition to reframing. The goal of mood management is to prevent negative emotions from dominating behavior and affecting one's health and well-being. Strong leaders do not allow their emotions to rule or dominate their reactions toward others.

3. Self-Motivation. Successful people have learned to marshal feelings of enthusiasm, zeal, and self-confidence, when needed. A common trait among all successful people, including Olympic athletes, world-class musicians, and chess grandmasters, is their ability to motivate themselves to pursue their goals and develop the needed discipline to reach those goals.

Psychologist Martin Seligman of the University of Pennsylvania advised the MetLife insurance company to hire a special group of job applicants who tested high on optimism, but had failed a normal aptitude test. When they were compared with salespeople who had passed the aptitude test but scored high in pessimism, the positive thinkers made 21 percent more sales the first year and 57 percent more in their second year.

Pessimistic people interpret events in a negative frame of reference. If they make a mistake, its because they never succeed in anything or it is someone's fault. Optimistic people interpret events from a more positive frame of reference. Instead of seeing mistakes as signs of failures, they see mistakes as opportunities to improve or learn something new. By not blaming failure on themselves, optimistic people are willing to try again and maybe a third or fourth time if necessary. When a leader is self-motivated, his/her enthusiasm and zeal become contagious.

4. Impulse Control. Twenty-first century leaders are people who have learned to delay impulsive behavior in order to reach a desired goal. In the 1960s, psychologist Walter Mischel conducted an interesting experiment with some preschool children at Stanford University.

Dr. Mischel told the children they could have a single marshmallow right now if they wanted one, or if they would wait while he ran an errand, they could have two marshmallows. Some of the children grabbed their marshmallow immediately, and some decided to wait, delaying gratification, until Dr. Mischel returned. The children who delayed gratification would cover their eyes, rest their heads on their arms, talk to themselves, even sing, in order to avoid the temptation. When Dr. Mischel returned, those children received two marshmallows.

Dr. Mischel followed up on those children who delayed gratification, and as adolescents they were more socially competent and self-assertive and better able to cope with the difficulties and frustrations of life. In contrast, the "one marshmallow" children became stubborn, indecisive, stressed adolescents.

The lesson: Your ability to set long-term goals and delay whatever impulses may appear at the moment that might hinder that goal, will help you reach the goal and find greater satisfaction in the process. So remember when you are faced with a decision that might interfere with your goal that a "one marshmallow" decision could affect the outcome of that goal. Outstanding leaders know how to set examples of delayed gratification that inspire others to follow through with their goals.

In addition to the above qualities of emotional intelligence, there is another skill necessary to becoming an effective leader: people skills.

People Skills

The second important area of leadership today is understanding people. The days are over when leaders were identified as the people who told others what to do and when to do it. Modern leaders know that the only way to have true success as a leader is not only to have a deep understanding of one's own emotional responses, but also to understand the needs and emotional responses of others. The key to successful leadership is to know as much about human nature as it is, not as the leader thinks it ought to be. Many have failed in leadership positions because they have tried to get people to respond the way the leaders thought the people should respond. One of the main problems in communications is people don't understand one another. Because of this lack of understanding, wars have been fought, societies have been destroyed, governments have toppled, religions have divided, and human lives have been wasted.

The Carnegie Institute of Technology did a research into the records of 10,000 persons and concluded that 15 percent of success is due to technical training (or just knowing how to do the job), and 85 percent is due to personality factors (the ability to get along with others). The Bureau of Vocational Guidance at Harvard University did a study of thousands of men and women who had lost jobs. They concluded that for every one person who lost his/her job because of failure to do the work correctly, two persons lost their jobs because of failure to deal with other people successfully. It is obvious from these studies, and many others like them, that the real need for today's leaders and managers is to understand people. That knowledge will set them apart as leaders.

Here are some important things to keep in mind about human beings.

1. The first basic principle: *All people are egotists.* That statement of fact should not be taken as a negative comment. It simply means all people are concerned with how they feel and what happens to them physically, mentally, emotionally, and spiritually. To say it another way, every person you meet wants to feel important and to feel he/she is a worthwhile person. Every person has a deep craving to be approved by others, to be liked by others. For some reason, most human beings have concluded that when others like them, they can like ourselves; when others accept them, they can accept ourselves.

Because of this deep need within each person to be liked and accepted, it can be said that most of us are "ego-hungry." Once this hunger is satisfied, we can then concentrate on helping others satisfy their hunger. So the person who likes himself or herself is better equipped to reach out and encourage others to like themselves. This is a basic truth that every effective leader understands.

The first law of effective leadership is to help people feel good about doing whatever it is you want them to do. In order for that to happen, you must appeal to their sense of worth and self-esteem. One of the best ways to accomplish this task is to realize that questions are interpersonal tools. Questions help you find out the needs and concerns of others and at the same time reduce their defensiveness. For example, instead of telling someone, "Here's what you must do," it would be better to ask, "Can I make some suggestions?" Their affirmative response gives you permission to provide guidance while at the same time protecting their ego.

I recently witnessed an event that illustrates how ineffective leadership fails to accomplish a desired task. I was checking out of a hotel, and the customer in front of me was checking in. He gave his name, and the young man checked the computer. After a moment or two, the young clerk said, "We don't seem to have your reservation; when did you make it?" The customer said he had made it several weeks ago and that he had requested a king-sized, nonsmoking room. After a few more minutes of searching the guest list, the young man said, "I'm sorry, but your name is not listed, and all we have is a twin-sized, smoking room." The man stiffened, cut his eyes away from the clerk and looked straight at the wall, with beads of sweat breaking out on his forehead and his face turning red (which was an indication of rising blood pressure), he said, "I cannot and I will not sleep in a twin-sized, smoking room!" All the physical signs suggested this person was experiencing great stress and anger at that moment over a situation that could have been handled much differently. The outcome was that the man had to take something less than what he had requested.

As I witnessed this event, it occurred to me that here is a situation which demands good leadership skills. One approach the man might have taken would have been to say, "Look, I know this is not your fault, but I made my reservation several weeks ago, and, because I am not in the computer, I have a real problem. I cannot sleep in a smoking room. You seem like a very capable person, so what can you do to help me out of this situation?" Now it may have been impossible for the young clerk to do anything about the situation, but it has been my experience with most hotels and motels that they keep a few rooms reserved for late arrivals, etc. In most cases, when approached with the right type of attitude, most hotel people will go to great lengths to help, if for no other reason than to maintain the self-esteem you have created within them with positive, self-affirming comments.

Research after research seems to validate this conclusion. Several surveys have revealed that the principal causes of unrest among workers are:

1. Failure to give credit for suggestions
2. Failure to correct grievances
3. Failure to encourage
4. Criticizing employees in front of other people
5. Failure to ask employees their opinions
6. Failue to inform employees of their progress
7. Favoritism

Each one of these is a failure to acknowledge the worth of the individual workers. Each says to the workers, "You nor your work is very important." So in order to prevent these things from happening with the people you are responsible for leading, here are three very important suggestions:

A. Recognize the intrinsic worth of every person. If you have problems believing each person is a worthy human being, then your attitude will be felt and "seen" in the ways you respond to the person you do not value as worthy. Granted, there are some people who, because of their life-choices, do not appear to be worthy of our respect. There are some people who have committed heinous crimes who do not deserve honor or respect from civilized society. But that fact does not diminish their intrinsic worth. Every living, breathing human being deserves to be respected as a human being. To do less is to disregard the value of another person. When you choose to disrespect another person, there is no way to make that person feel important or significant. Any efforts to counter your negative feelings will only be forms of manipulation which, in the end, will fail.

Dr. J. B. Rhine of Duke University in his book *The Reach of the Mind* (New York: William Sloane Associates, Inc., 1947) made this observation:

> *"Our treatment of people obviously depends on what we think they are, as does our treatment of everything else. No other way would be intelligent. Our feelings for men* [and women, too—this was written before gender-free writing evolved, BRS] *depend on our ideas, our knowledge about them. The more we are led on the one hand to think of our fellowmen as deterministic physical systems—robots, machines, brains—the more heartlessly and selfishly we can allow ourselves to deal with them.*

> *"On the other hand, the more we appreciate their mental life as something unique in nature, something more original and creative than the mere space-time-mass relations of matter, the more we are interested in them as individuals, and the more we tend to respect them and consider their viewpoints and feelings.*

> *Our interpersonal dealings are elevated to a level of mutual interest, of understanding, of fellowship."*

Even though written in the late '40s, that statement is as up-to-date as tomorrow's newspapers. Successful Twenty-first century leaders realize the truthfulness of this statement more today than when it was written.

B. Be a global thinker. A global thinker is a leader who not only respects the worth of each person, but also has become culturally sensitive. American businesses are now developing operations in Prague, Ho Chi Minh City, and Beijing, as well as every other major city of the world. We now talk in terms of the Global Village or the Global Community, referring to the entire planet earth as one large community made up of diverse people and cultures. A leader's ability to deal with differences in nationality, race, ethnicity, gender, disability, and religion will be a critical part of his/her success in the twenty-first century.

Becoming a global thinker means more than just respecting the intrinsic worth of another person, it means treating that person with fairness and equality and recognizing that he/she has skills and knowledge that can make real and profitable contributions to our global society. These types of leaders are able to tap into the world brain pool and draw creative thinking and problem-solving techniques from the variety of cultures represented in the global village today. These leaders do not engage in what I call "one-culture thinking," the idea that only one culture (the one represented by the leader) is the only culture that is capable of *real* thinking and reasoning. Rather, global leaders recognize the value of a multicultural workforce and are able, because of their respect for each individual, to utilize the talents, abilities, education, and skills of this incredible variety of people represented in this global society.

A visit to Silicon Valley would reveal the truthfulness of the above observation. Any company in the Valley that you might choose to visit will be made up of people not only from the United States, but also Romania, Japan, China, Tonga, South Korea, all parts of Asia, and all of them are working together. The demographers are estimating that by the year 2050, more than 60 percent of the U.S. workforce will be people of color. Almost half will be women! What a tremendous opportunity this workforce presents to those leaders who recognize the power and potential in such a diversity of people.

These leaders live by our national identity: *E pluribus unum* . . . "Out of the many, one."

C. Be a lifelong learner. Twenty-first-century leaders realize that learning is a lifetime experience. Lifelong learners are always striving for constant and never-ending improvement. By dedicating one's life to constant learning and improving, the leader inspires and encourages others to follow his/her example of growth and development. At the same time, the leader continues to learn more and more about human nature and how to provide for the emotional and psychological needs of the employees.

Many corporations have learned the importance of lifelong learning and have developed or are in the process of developing the concept of becoming a "learning organization." Learning organizations are dedicated to training and developing their employees so the employees can continue to improve their abilities not only in their areas of expertise, but also in other areas as well. This will make the employees more valuable to the organization, and the organization is better equipped to challenge the competition with better products and customer service. But one of the greatest advantages of the concept of lifelong learning is the worth that the organization communicates to the employee. In times past, many people have felt no one really cared for them. But learning organizations are communicating a different message to the employees; it is a message of value and worth, demonstrated by the investment of time, money, and energy in the employees' development and growth.

One example of this type of employee development is the Arkansas Eastman branch of Eastman, Inc. Here is their document entitled: *Expectations for Lifelong Learning.*

> *All employees are expected to contribute to self-improvement, as well as team and business improvement. Eastman hires people*

to improve the making of products and the providing of services, not just to make products and provide services. Long term, the success of the company and the well being of Arkansas Eastman people depend on continual improvement. This necessitates continuous learning throughout an employee's career.

As reflected in the principles of "The Eastman Way" and "The Eastman Quality Policy," Arkansas Eastman is committed to providing an environment of lifelong learning and development. This commitment is supported by the Employee Development System and training processes which assist individuals, teams, and organizations in enhancing skills to meet the challenges of an increasingly competitive and technical world.

It is Arkansas Eastman's expectation that all employees pursue opportunities for lifelong learning and development. Accordingly, employees are expected too:

- Understand the business of objectives of their team/organization and how they can contribute to meeting these objectives.
- Assume personal responsibility for learning; identify what they are responsible for and seek ways to improve business results.
- Utilize the EDS process to identify and achieve personal learning and development opportunities.
- Be open to learning through others; be receptive to feedback, inquiry and dialogue; be willing to explore new ideas; and freely share ideas and expertise with others.
- Treat mistakes by self and others as opportunities to learn; analyze mistakes to identify system-related causes, not to place blame.

Employees in jobs with formalized training or apprentice programs are expected to enroll in and complete the applicable program(s) in a reasonable timeframe as determined by departmental management teams. As apprentice programs are upgraded, or as employees change areas or departments, employees are expected to complete the applicable new or revised program.

The expectations for lifelong learning exist for management, as well as non-management employees. Managers have an additional responsibility for:

- *Creating and nurturing a learning environment in their team/organization.*
- *Ensuring their team/organization is focused on the important improvement and learning issues for company success.*
- *Utilizing the EDS process to help employees in their team/organization successfully achieve learning opportunities and expectations.*
- *Reinforcing learning behaviors for team/organization members.*

This is one of the best documents I have ever read defining lifelong learning within an organization. Obviously, the management and leaders in such an organization must set the examples and demonstrate the benefit of lifelong learning for the employees. This is one of the key areas for managers and supervisors in the twenty-first century. The value this places on each employee, and the development of a higher level of self-esteem, cannot be measured in dollars and cents. The employee becomes more valuable to himself or herself and thus more valuable to the organization.

2. The second basic principle to keep in mind: *People have feelings.* In addition to the fact that all people are egotists, it is vitally important to recognize the fact that people have feelings, and those feelings are constantly controlling and motivating people at any given moment of the day or night. This is, in fact, an extension of emotional intelligence and is a necessary part of good people skills.

To be able to know how a person feels is important in every relationship in life, whether that relationship be a romance, marriage, friendship, family, or business. Human beings transmit and receive moods and feelings in subtle ways on an almost imperceptible level. For example, the way a person says "hello" can communicate appreciation, patronization, or rejection. When a person is capable of discerning the feelings behind other people's words, body language, etc., that person can also control his or her own signals. The result is better communication between individuals and better cooperation and response to one another.

Robert Kelley of Carnegie-Mellon University and Janet Caplan in a study at Bells Labs in Naperville, Ill., demonstrated the importance of "networking" feelings. The labs were staffed by engineers and scientists with high IQs. Some of the engineers and scientists were highly successful while others seemed to falter. Kelley and Caplan did their research to determine why some highly intelligent people succeed and other highly intelligent people fail. Here is what they found.

The top performers had a network of friends who would respond to their requests for help, etc. The less-successful performers had not developed the network of friends, thus when they requested help, there was little or no response from others. This research project demonstrated the importance of "networking" before the need arises for help. The key to networking is the ability to "connect" with other people, not only on a surface level, but also on an emotional level.

The successful leader has the ability to appreciate the feelings of others and is able to connect with people in ways that communicate understanding, sympathy, patience, and trust. The result is a positive response from those who feel understood.

The ability to not only understand and control one's own emotions, but also to connect with others emotionally are the two important characteristics that twenty-first-century leaders must develop in order to meet the demands of a society that is gaining more understanding of what makes people "tick." In summary, here is a list of qualities that describe the overall characteristics of twenty-first-century leaders:

    1. They listen with an open mind to others.

2. They delegate and enable others to act.
3. They have goals, imagination, and vision.
4. They show enthusiasm, drive, determination.
5. They serve as a role model for the ideals, they believe in: honesty, common sense, hard work.
6. They respect individuals and build self-esteem.
7. They show praise and believe in themselves, so they don't "have something to prove to others."
8. They empathize and encourage.
9. They have the energy to make things happen.
10. They are slow to criticize, quick to praise.

Chapter 8

How to Communicate with Outstanding Customer Service

This chapter is about E-Plus thinking: Exceptional customer service that exceeds the customer's expectations in positive ways. Today's business is a consumer-driven environment. There is more power in the hands of the customer today than ever before. Yet, in many cases, the service given to the customer is far less than the customer expects.

In order to understand what exceptional customer service really means, I want to begin with a description of professionalism which lays a groundwork for this chapter:

I will do the best I can. I will give my full attention to what I am trying to accomplish in each moment and not half-do what needs to be fully done or put off until later what must be done now.

I will know everything I need to know. I will prepare myself to be knowledgeable about my company, my products, my customers, my competition, and my marketplace.

I will continuously try to improve. I will always seek knowledge and continue to study to raise my knowledge levels, and I will use self-analysis to correct my weakness and improve my strength.

I will be able to replicate performance. I will practice my performance until I am able to repeat it perfectly without deviation.

I will not let my feelings inhibit my success. I will perform at high levels as needed in spite of required repetitions and emotional distractions.

I will set performance goals and make plans to achieve them. I will prioritize what I do to concentrate on those activities that contribute to goal achievement and modify my plans as necessary to adapt to changing conditions in order to meet my goals.(author unknown)

These are the E-Plus qualities of a professional who will be able to provide E-Plus customer service. There is no more challenging area of communication than customer service. To be good at providing effective customer service, one must be able to communicate well, keep emotions under control, think about what is best for the customer, listen carefully and with empathy, and most of all... care about the customer's needs and wants. These skills are in great demand in today's consumer-driven marketplace.

It seems important that a good definition be given to the word "customer." Dick Schaaf (*Keeping the Edge, Giving Customers the Service they Demand*) defines customer as someone with the ability and the willingness to buy or not buy something. That seems to be a good, workable definition. Some people may not want the product or service, or may not have the ability to buy the product or service. A true customer has both the ability and the willingness.

Customer Service: A Definition

It's important to define the meaning of customer service: *Customer Service means all features, acts, and information that augment the customer's ability to realize the potential value of a core product or service.* Today a business is not defined by the company's name, mission statement, or articles of incorporation. It is defined by the needs and wants the customer satisfies upon buying a product or service. The purpose of every business today is to satisfy the customer by giving *value* to the product or service. Sometimes that value is perceived as getting something the customer did not pay for, or it may be little things like someone calling the customer by name, or a smile, or solving a little problem. Value is that extra something that helps the customer to realize how valuable the product or service is, and when that value is given, it can, in many cases, prevent customer remorse (the regret that sets in after the product or service is purchased).

To better understand *value*, it is important to understand that customers don't buy products or services, they buy what products and services can *do* for them. Ron Willingham, in his book *Hey, I'm the Customer,* gives a partial list of why people buy things:

- to be entertained
- to receive pleasure
- to enjoy peace of mind
- to receive recognition
- to economize or save money
- to impress others
- to have better health
- to promote friendship or family togetherness
- to gratify their own egos
- to prevent future losses
- to acquire or possess

Businesses today must move from product based to customer based thinking. In order for that to happen, each business must understand the "Total Product Concept." Devised by Theodore Levitt, professor of Harvard Business School, "Total Product Concept" includes all services and features that accompany the product, such as delivery, payment terms, technical support or repairs, installation, maintenance, spare parts, packaging, and the like. It includes all the "extras" that make the product or service attractive to the customer. As these extras are added to new products or services, the expectation level of the customer continues to rise. The way a company defines its product depends on the total package of benefits the customer receives when the product or service is purchased. In order to help define the total product concept, here are some important questions that each business should be able to answer:

1. What are our principle products or services?
2. What are some possible substitutes for these?
3. Why do customers buy these products or services?

4. What are the principal benefits the customers expect from these products or services?
5. What needs/wants do customers satisfy by buying these products or services?
6. What problems do the customers solve with these products or services.

Once these questions are asked and answered, then it's time to move to a deeper understanding of what E-plus customer service really means. The remainder of this chapter will answer that question.

The Dissatisfied Customer

The dissatisfied customer can be a challenge, but also an opportunity. The challenge comes in meeting the customer's needs, the opportunity comes from learning how to satisfy a customer and also to discover a potential hidden problem with a product or service. Paul R. Timm, in his book *50 Powerful Ideas You Can Use to Keep Your Customers,* gives some important things to keep in mind about the dissatisfied customer:

1. The customer wants to be heard and taken seriously.
2. The customer wants someone to understand the problem and the reason for being upset.
3. The customer wants either compensation and/or restitution.
4. The customer wants the problems handled *quickly.*
5. The customer does not want to be inconvenienced any further.
6. The customer wants respect.
7. The customer may want someone to be punished for the problem.
8. The customer wants assurance the problem will not happen again.

It is commonly understood that one dissatisfied customer will tell ten or eleven others about the bad experience. But with the

Internet, you can multiply that figure by thousands. There are several newsgroups on the Net where consumers trade information about the treatment they've received from companies. Now a customer who feels ripped off or mistreated doesn't have to settle for telling ten or eleven people, he or she can now broadcast the story to thousands. This is the one way the customer can "get even" for the feeling of being cheated. It is something companies should take into consideration.

In addition, it costs five to ten times as much to get a new customer as to maintain an existing one. So most companies will not lose much by going the extra mile to meet the demands or needs of a dissatisfied customer.

A study published a few years ago by the Technical Assistance Research Programs Institute revealed this interesting statistic. Ninety-five (95) percent of unhappy customers never complain to the company, they just silently go away to a competitor. The reasons customers do not complain can be as varied as the individual customers, but some obvious reasons are:

1. Some believe that complaining will do no good. They know there is very little most employees can do about the situation, so why bother? It is must easier to switch than fight. Since competition has provided so many options, it is much easier to take one's business elsewhere than to complain.

2. It is difficult to complain. There are usually several steps a customer has to go through in order to complain. For one thing, the customer has to find someone "in charge" who can resolve the issue. That person is usually not available immediately; therefore, the customer has to get the address, write a complaint letter, and then wait several weeks to get a resolution.

3. It is embarrassing for some customers to complain. It's uncomfortable to approach another person and possibly ruin his/her day with a complaint. There are a few customers who seem to enjoy upsetting others with gripes

and complaints, but many would rather go away in silence.

The good news is, when a complaint is registered and resolved, seventy percent will do business with the company again. That figure climbs to ninety-five percent if the customer feels the complaint was solved quickly. Once the complaint is resolved, the customer will tell an average of five people about the good treatment.

In view of the above statistics, here are some important suggestions that will help in communicating effectively with the customer.

1. Listen carefully without interrupting. Allow the customer to finish each thought. A good guideline is to count to three before saying anything after the customer stops talking.
2. Agree with the customer's right to complain. Regardless of whether you agree with the customer, realize he/she has a right not to like the service received or the product which was purchased.
3. Listen for and acknowledge their emotions. Watching the body language and expressions on the face, as well as listening for the words, will reveal the emotions at the moment. When a particular emotion is noted, express empathy at that time. "I can see how that would upset you." "I know it is frustrating to have to spend time trying to solve this issue."
4. Repeat their words back. "What I understand you to be saying is . . . . " This one skill can communicate value to the customer.
5. Find a place to apologize. One of the most important things to apologize for is the inconvenience caused by the problem.
6. Thank the customer for telling you about the problem. Let him/her know the problem is not an inconvenience, but rather an opportunity to not only correct a problem, but also to improve your service.

7. Then take action. Either solve the problem immediately, or put the customer in contact with whoever has the authority to solve the problem.

Throughout the whole process, do everything possible to make the customer feel valued and important. If for some reason the customer's complaint cannot be solved the way the customer demands, then give the customer something of equal value or importance. Remember, not only does your business's reputation rest on how well the problem is solved, but also it can be costly not to solve the problem to the customer's satisfaction.

At this point it would be helpful to understand why customers buy products and services:

- Some people buy what they want regardless of price.
- Some people will purchase things only because the price is high.
- Some people will purchase what they don't need if the price is right.
- Some people will not purchase what they want if the price is too high.
- Some people want what they don't need and don't want what they do need.
- Some people want what is bad for them.

Consequently, when customers are dissatisfied, there is perhaps a combination of the above reasons for buying the product/service. It becomes obvious, in some cases, as to why the customer is dissatisfied. Once the reason is discovered, the customer service personnel can lead the customer to a decision that would be in the best interest of the customer. Sometimes refunding the money is the simplest way to satisfy a customer who has bought a product that is not needed.

The obvious question may arise here: How can I know if my customers are being satisfied? Here are some guidelines that will help answer that question:

1. Are your customers making repeat purchases?

2. Are your customers purchasing new products and new services that have made them happy in the past?
3. Are your customers giving referrals? Remember, referrals represent active loyalty.
4. Are the personal relationships between your employees and your customers so strong that your customers would feel as though they're leaving family to go elsewhere?

The Customer is Always Right

H. Gordon Selfridge, the junior partner of Marshall Field, is believed to be the person who originated the use of "the customer is always right." From one perspective, that slogan is right. Because even when the customer is wrong, to refuse the customer's demands and requests may result in the loss of business that could cost much more than the original request the customer made. So to meet the customer's demands could mean not only satisfying the customer, but also saving the money that would be involved in gaining a new customer to replace the dissatisfied customer. In that sense, the customer is "right."

In another sense, however, the customer is usually wrong because of unreasonable expectations. Fred Jandt, in his book *The Customer is Usually Wrong*, observes, "The simple truth is that today all too many service encounters are not satisfying to either the customer or the service provider. The key to that dissatisfaction is unrealistic expectations. Customers are not getting what they expect, and front-line service providers don't have enough authority or training to deal with those unrealistic expectations."

The University of Michigan Business School created the American Customer Satisfaction Index (ACSI) about three years ago. The index is based on regular interviews with 16,000 customers of about 200 companies in 33 industries. The interviews revealed a declining satisfaction with service in each quarter since it began. On a scale of 1 to 100, the ACSI shows that overall opinion of service customers received has dropped steadily from 74.5 in 1994 to 70.7 in 1997.

What is strange about the above statistics is that during that same period of time, a great deal of emphasis was put on the importance of good customer service in books by Peter Drucker, Tom Peters, Brian Tracy, et al. The result of all this emphasis on customer service is the public became more educated in what to expect from their service providers and retail stores. But at the same time, many companies were downsizing, re-engineering, and replacing workers with machines, which is usually not an option for customer service. However, some companies like FedEx, UPS, and Nordstrom's were keeping their customers happy despite the new pressures to follow the lead of other organizations.

The result of all this has been a better educated consumer who expects companies to provide service which may be impossible for them to deliver. Therefore, the customer is wrong because the expectation level has risen above that which the average store, product, or service can provide. But whether right or wrong, the customer is still the customer, a fact that must never be forgotten by any business that wants to succeed in today's highly competitive marketplace.

Begin a Customer-Obsessed Movement

In every organization or business, there must be a culture developed in which the customer is viewed by everyone (custodian to CEO) as the most valuable asset the business or organization owns. Tom Peters (*Thriving on Chaos,* p.108) writes:

> *When the Federal Express courier enters my office, she should see $180,000 stamped on the forehead of our receptionist. My little twenty-five-person firm runs about a $1,500 -a-month Fed Ex bill. Over ten years, that will add up to $180,000. I suggest that this simple device, calculating the ten-year (or, alternatively, lifetime) value of a customer can be very powerful—and has sweeping implications.*

> *Grocer Stew Leonard got me started on this. He says, 'When I see a frown on a customer's face, I see $50,000 about to walk out the door. His good customers buy about $100 worth of groceries a week. Over ten years, that adds up to roughly*

$50,000. We all agree that repeat trade is the key to business success. This simple quantifying device provides a way to add potency to the idea.

Here are two other examples. Average lifetime auto purchases will total about $150,000, not including repair work. Given the remarkably low dealer loyalty of car buyers these days, might it not make a difference if dealers and their employees focused on this big number? Or suppose you frequent a good restaurant twice a month for a six-person business dinner. You're worth about $75,000 every ten years to that establishment.

Suppose a lifelong, happy customer sells just one colleague on becoming a lifelong customer of your fine restaurant, grocery store or Federal Express, as the case may be. Suddenly, the regular customer's value to the restaurant doubles from $75,000 to $150,000, including that likely word-of-mouth referral. And that sign on my receptionist's forehead should now be read by the Fed Ex person as $360,000 rather than $180,000.

If the restaurant's waiter handles five tables a night, he or she is catering to 5 x $150,000, or $750,000, worth of potential business. The numbers are stunning for Fed Ex. If our courier has forty regular stops at businesses my size (which would be normal), she is managing each day a 'portfolio' of customers worth 40 x $360,000, or $14 million, to Federal Express!

The implications of the above examples are clear. You can calculate the value of your individual customer the same way. Just estimate the ten-year or lifelong value of a customer, based on the average amount of each customer's transaction. Multiply that number by two, to take into account the possibility of that customer leading one other person to become a lifetime customer. Then multiply that total by the average number of customers served per day by your sales, service, or front-line people. The result is the lifelong value of your customer base. Once these numbers tell you the value of each customer, then it is time to begin a customer-obsessed movement within your company.

The first step in this movement is to hire your customer-contact people very carefully.

Hiring Customer-Loving People

What things should you look for in the people you hire? Here are a few suggestions for selecting your "point of encounter" employees:

1. Hire people who are goal oriented. Ask about their goals to determine if the goals are attainable and ambitious.
2. Look for self-confidence, self-respect, honesty, high integrity, and general good judgment.
3. Determine their attitude toward other people. Find out if they respect people from different cultures, races, religions, etc. Hire for attitude and train for aptitude!
4. Find out about any experience and/or education that has prepared them for the job of meeting people and helping them with their problems, etc.
5. One key area is their willingness and ability to take on responsibility for their actions and results.
6. Finally, hire people who like people! There is no other choice. When you hire people who like people, your customers will notice!

After the person is hired and trained, continue to communicate the importance of excellent customer service. Here are some suggestions as to how that can be done:

1. Continue to let them know what is expected of them, that is, to treat the customer as they would like to be treated by putting the customer's needs first and foremost.
2. Promote life long learning and continuous education. Provide seminars, reading material, videos, in-house training on customer service. Make sure *every* employee is acquainted with Peter Drucker, Tom Peters, Brian Tracy, et al.
3. Treat the employees like customers!

4. Let the employees know "what's in it for me?" Remind them of such things as pride, satisfaction, a positive environment, the carry-over value to future jobs, the continuing challenge that keeps their jobs interesting, interpersonal skills that help develop their personality, and knowledge about customer/client relationship, which is often more important than money in so far as future job security and professional growth.

These guidelines can help in hiring and training people to handle your most valuable asset... your customers. As the employee is being trained, it is important to instill in that person the idea that he/she is working for the customer first and the company second. Serving the customer well is also serving the company well. Without the customer, there is no company or business! The orientation and training process should include the following:

Welcoming the new employee, giving a history of the organization and introducing him/her into the culture of excellent customer service.

Orienting the new employee to the job and how it relates to customer service.

Training the new employee in the skills, attitudes, and expectations of the job.

Transitioning the new employee from trainee to a fully functioning, successful customer-centered professional.

Creating a Customer-Centered Culture

The word "culture" describes the atmosphere that permeates your business. It should be one of total customer care. It's a set of values, attitudes, and ways of doing things to benefit the customer. The word "culture" refers to "rules of behavior, written or unwritten," that the entire organization is expected to live by. There must be continuous improvement of value-adding processes beginning with Research and Development, and following through Production, Sales, Distribution, and Service. Every person on the entire team must realize the value and importance of each customer that buys and uses the product or service. So how do you move in that direction? Tom Peters and Nancy Austin, in their book *A Passion for Excellence*, make the following suggestions:

1. Company bulletins, annual reports and all other forms of printed matter feature stories about working with customers.
2. In a host of ways, unique respect for salespeople is demonstrated.
3. Customer support people are showered with attention.
4. The importance of the customer pervades every function of the organization. The customer is "alive," through displays of letters (good and bad), film clips and visits, and what-have-you in MIS, accounting, personnel and legal, as well as in the main-line and direct customer support functions.
5. There is a special (and friendly/respectful) language associated with customers. (Disney calls them "Guests," People Express calls them "customers" rather than "Passengers.")
6. Reviews and reports of all kinds have a disproportionate share of their content aimed at customers and revenue-enhancement activities.
7. Visits with customers are exchanged regularly, at all levels in the company and customer organization.
8. Hallway discussions, celebration of heroes—minor and major—overwhelmingly (again, by actual count) focus on support for the customer.
9. Devices abound for customer listening (surveys, various ways of feedback, request forms, etc.).
10. Customer satisfaction is measured frequently—monthly at least, and perhaps as often as weekly.
11. Devices exist to ensure that connections are made (and then acted upon) between sales and engineering and manufacturing.

12. "Overkill" complaint response mechanisms are firmly locked in place so every level of management is aware of a "foul up" with a customer.
13. Promises to customers are kept, period, regardless of cost in overtime.
14. The calendars of executives at all levels and in all functions reflect their insistent focus on customers.
15. Quality and reliability of product and service is an obsession throughout the organization, reflecting virtually the same intensity as that directed to the customer *per se*.
16. Every element of the organization actively looks for ways that it can specifically contribute to differentiating the product or service. Even small, minuscule improvements are rewarded.
17. Manufacturers (or operations people in service companies) are deeply involved in customer activities, especially selling (directly) and joint problem-solving teams.
18. The customer's perception is what's viewed as important, rather than so-called hard-nosed view reality.
19. There is an explicit philosophy statement, part of or an adjunct to the corporate philosophy statement, that deals with "the way we perceive and treat customers."
20. Executives (and managers at all levels) from all functions regularly spend time performing all primary customer-support tasks—e.g., working on the loading dock, at the dispatch center, in the spares department, at the distribution center.
21. Executives in all functions keep track of and manage the bureaucratic (e.g., paperwork) load that gets in the way of customer-contact time for all customer-related functions—e.g., reception, sales, field, service, dispatch. "Time in front of (or in direct support of) the customer" is guarded and tracked jealously/measured religiously.
22. The number one "it" is a passion for tiny customer-related improvements in every department.

Strive to be the best by following these suggestions. Any organization can be the best of its kind, but the key is to know that improvement is needed on an ongoing basis.

Identifying Marks of Service Quality

Texas A & M University did an extensive research project on service quality and identified five dimensions that would identify and provide outstanding service to every customer:

Reliability= Deliver what is promised.

Assurance= The ability to convey trust and confidence.

Tangibles= The physical facilities, and the appearance of the employees.

Empathy= The ability to care.

These are things customers look for in the organizations with which they choose to do business. So here are some suggestions on how to communicate these qualities to the customers:

1. Give every customer a sincere smile. This is a big "tangible."
2. Create a relaxed, open posture that communicates reliability.
3. Lean slightly toward the customer, which communicates care and concern.
4. Maintain eye contact, which communicates self-confidence and gives assurance to the customer.
5. Remember the customer's name, it communicates a degree of empathy or caring.
6. Mirror the customer's behavior (i.e., rate of speech, tone of voice, posture), so the customer can feel at ease.

This chapter contains some wonderful information on how to effectively communicate to your customers in a way that can produce incredible growth within your organization. As a final thought, here are some suggestions that will give your organization an extra bonus in good customer service:

- Develop a customer profile so you can know who your customers are (age, income level, needs, etc.)
- Look at your business through your customer's eyes. Take a visual inventory to determine what the customer thinks when he/she enters your store the first time or looks at your product.
- Don't overpromise and undersell. This will cause the customer to feel shortchanged and produce "buyer's remorse."
- Look at customer complaints and problems as opportunities to grow, improve, become better at satisfying needs.
- Treat each customer as a special person, with special needs who could become a lifelong customer.
- Stay in touch and keep your customers informed (phone calls, letters, brochures, newsletters, etc.).

William Siefkin, manager of the sales-development program at E. I. du Pont de Nemours & Company, said,

> "The biggest challenge is to really bring the voice of the customer into your company, so that the customer is at every meeting in some way and so that our guidance comes from them when we're trying to make the decisions" (*The Customer Driven Company*, p. 183).

Here are the key words that in one way or another describe excellent customer service:

- Rewarding
- Solving
- Saving
- Empathizing
- Reassuring
- Complimenting
- Giving something extra
- Expressing kindness!

Chapter 9

How to Communicate with Good Health and Nutrition

It may seem strange to find a chapter on health and nutrition in a book on communication. But with a little thought on the matter, it is easy to see how these topics are a very important part of good communication. As you have already learned in previous chapters, a great deal of our communication takes place through our bodies. Over ninety percent of our communication is nonverbal (facial expressions, body language, sound of voice). What we say with our bodies, therefore, is vitally important. When our bodies are in good shape, healthy, and strong, we communicate to others good self-esteem, confidence, strength, and self-control. These positive messages are a part of our self-image and they tell others a great deal about how we feel about ourselves and how we feel about them. A person who cares enough about himself/herself to eat right, exercise, and stay in good health can give more attention, love, and care to others. The reason is obvious: A person who does not feel well or operates on a low-energy level or is in poor health, certainly does not have the strength and energy to give attention and care to others. Therefore, good health and proper nutrition can make a tremendous difference in how well one communicates.

There are three areas in which attention must be given in order to maintain good health: exercise, diet/nutrition, and stress. In this chapter we'll look at each.

Exercise

There is no other single thing a person can do to improve quality of life and health more than to exercise. Dr. Roy Shepard, M.D., Ph.D., professor of applied physiology at the University of Toronto, says, "By taking yourself from a sedentary state to a physically trained state, you can, in effect, reduce your biological age by 10 to 20 years." If exercise could be bottled and sold as a prescription, it would be the best selling "medicine" of all time because of the energy, health, and overall good feeling it produces. Unfortunately, in order to enjoy these benefits of exercise, there must be more effort involved than opening a bottle and swallowing a pill!

Evidence in favor of good physical conditioning and exercise and the effect it has on aging is almost overwhelming. For example, researchers have measured the effects of aging on 756 athletes, ages 35 to 94. These athletes participated in a variety of sports such as rowing, swimming, and track and field during the 1985 World Masters Games. "We found some people in their late 60s and 70s who had about the same cardiopulmonary fitness as you would expect from sedentary 25-year-olds," says Terence Kavanagh, M.D., director of the Toronto Rehabilitation Centre.

One study of 16,936 Harvard University alumni, ages 35 to 74, was conducted by Stanford University researchers. This study covered a period of about 15 years. Death rates were up to one-third (33%) lower among those alumni who burned an average of 2,000 or more calories a week in some form of exercise. In order to burn an average of 2,000 calories per week, one would need to run or walk about three miles per day. And it is never too late to start exercising and gaining benefits from it. Research has shown that people between the ages of 35-55 can add about two years to their life expectancy, and even people in their 70s can add six months to their lifespan with an exercise program that burns around 2,000 calories per week.

Of course, exercise alone will not help much. There must also be a healthy lifestyle that would include maintaining ideal weight, eating the right foods; refraining from smoking, fatty foods, and alcohol; keeping the cholesterol low; and supplementing with vitamins and minerals. When all of these are combined, one can expect to live an energetic, productive, disease-free, and stress-free life.

Aging is biological to some degree. We inherit a part of our lifespan from the genes of our forebears. All of us are programmed to live up to a certain number of years (usually somewhere between 65-100). But a part of aging is also self-inflicted. A person in poor physical condition tires easily, is able to do less, is mentally sluggish (because of the reduction of oxygen to the brain), and is less capable of enjoying the advantages of life in this world. The consequences of this lifestyle are often depression, anxiety, stress, frustration, unhappiness, and low self-esteem. These are the causes of poor health and heart disease, which is the number one killer in the U.S. today.

Where does one begin? The first step is one of common sense. Just look around at the people who are able to work harder, tire less, and enjoy their lives more. These will generally be the people who are in good physical and mental condition. So this becomes the inspiration to improve life. Without this inspiration, there will be very little motivation to change one's habits.

The second step is to begin slowly with any kind of aerobic exercise: brisk walking, slow running, swimming, cycling. Whatever the exercise, be sure there is some huffing and puffing. The more one huffs and puffs, the more oxygen is going into the body and, consequently, the better the body performs. Set a goal to perform this exercise three times a week for about 30 minutes. Within about four weeks, you will begin to notice a difference in your energy level, the quality of your sleep, your mental alertness, and overall well-being.

In order to develop sufficient and safe cardiovascular training, you must hit what is called the "Target Zone." The Target Zone varies according to age. The minimal target is 70 percent of one's maximum heart rate, and the cut-off figure is 85 percent of one's maximum heart rate. To exercise below these numbers will not provide the needed aerobic or cardiovascular exercise needed for good fitness.

Here is how you can determine your training heart-rate range. Subtract your age from 220. The minimum for your heart rate is 70 percent of this number, and your maximum rate is 85 percent. Here is a chart to help with your computation:

Age	70% Minimum Rate	85% Maximum Rate
20-25	140	167
26-30	134	163
31-35	131	159
36-40	127	155
41-45	124	150
46-50	120	146
51-55	117	142
56-60	113	138
61-65	110	133
66-70	106	129

If you don't have a heart monitor, use the "talk test." If your are walking at a brisk pace, or running so fast you cannot carry on a conversation, you have probably exceeded your maximum level. However, if the exercise does not cause you to break a sweat, or produce some huffing and puffing, you probably have not reached your minimum level of exercise. Of course, one way to check your aerobic level is to check your pulse while you are walking or running; however, it is a little difficult to do while swimming! The bottom line is to listen to your body. It will let you know if you are pushing too hard, so back down when you are feeling breathless or fatigued. Your exercise program should be fun, not stressful or strenuous.

My favorite exercise is running; I started running when I was around 43. It has been one of the most beneficial things I have ever done for myself. I have been able to lose weight and maintain my desired weight level. I have had more energy, mental alertness, and better sleep as a result of my running. I have also noticed my stress level dropping considerably. My outlook on life has been more positive, as well. One reason for these changes is that exercise-induced mental and physiological changes, including the flood of body-made opiates that produce what has been called the "runner's high," can create a change in consciousness. When running, I feel a kind of expansiveness, an integration with my environment... the trees, hills, valleys, meadows, ocean, buildings, etc. As the air enters my lungs, there is a feeling of continuity between the air inside and outside. Yogis would call this feeling a unity of one's true state of existence, a oneness with the world. Whatever it is called, running has provided for me a way to live my life with discipline, peace, thoughtfulness, and remarkable insightfulness. It is as much a part of my life today as eating, sleeping, and breathing.

But running does not have to be your thing. Whatever exercise you choose, pick one you enjoy and one that expresses your true feelings about yourself and about the person you really want to become.

Nutrition

There is a revolution going on today in the health care industry. For generations, doctors have prepared themselves to cure disease and illness. In so doing, they have focused on the symptoms of disease: fevers, headaches, rashes, diminished energy, etc. Once a disease is diagnosed, it is treated with a synthetic medicine or perhaps invasive surgery in an effort to remove it from the body.

The problem facing modern medicine is most major illnesses such as heart disease, cancer, diabetes, and more, cannot be cured by medicines and surgeries. For this reason, many people have decided it is much wiser to prevent a disease rather than trying to find a cure after the disease has taken hold of the body. So the movement toward preventive medicine and nutritional health care is growing by leaps and bounds today.

Countless studies and research tell us if we maintain good health, we have a better chance of never getting sick in the first place. More and more medical professionals agree that maintaining the proper balance of nutrients in the body is essential to preventative health care.

Where It All Begins

The human body is made up of trillions of cells, each one working round the clock ingesting and digesting nutrients, producing energy, removing wastes, and reproducing so the body can perform all its functions. Our bodies work similar to our car engines: We take in fuel and oxygen and expend energy.

The secrets to good health and aging lie deep in the molecular biology of our cells. When our cells are healthy, they reproduce healthy cells, and our bodies function to their fullest capacities. But there are potential enemies inside our bodies called free radicals.

Free radicals are oxygen molecules with a missing or unpaired electron which spins erratically throughout the body, damaging every cell and tissue it contacts until it is finally stopped by an antioxidant. Some very powerful antioxidants are vitamin C or E, beta-carotene, bioflavonoids, or certain enzymes produced by the body.

Here is how the process works. A normal oxygen atom has four parts of electrons. As the body goes through a normal oxygen metabolism process (or exposure to certain chemicals and pollutants in the environment, as well as sunlight, radiation, burns, cigarette smoke, drugs, alcohol, viruses, bacterial, parasites, dietary fats, and many other things), one or more of the atom's electrons may separate from the oxygen atom. This atom, now missing an electron, tries to replace it by raiding other molecules. It is now a free radical, and will take electrons from other molecules in a cell wall damaging them in the process, and causing a chain reaction. Free radicals can destroy cell membranes, damage collagen and other connective tissue, disrupt important physiological processes, and create mutations in the DNA of cells. It is believed free radicals are the cause of many diseases, including heart attacks, hardening of the arteries, arthritis, Alzheimer's disease, cataracts, and cancer of all kinds.

Over the years, these free radicals can produce an enormous amount of cellular damage until the totality of destruction reaches a point of no return. The cells of the body are no longer fit to reproduce or even stay alive and function normally. This is the process we call aging.

The culprit in all this is the very breath of life: oxygen. Every breath of life we breathe ultimately produces oxygen atoms in the body that turn into free radicals. There is some good news/bad news here, because we need the free radicals to fight infection, ironically. Jean Carper, in her book *Stop Aging Now!*, writes, "When the body mobilizes to fight off infectious agents, it generates a burst of free radicals to destroy the invaders very efficiently. On the other hand, free radicals, including the pervasive superoxides created by respirations, careen out of control through the body, attacking cells, turning their fats rancid, rusting their proteins, piercing their membranes and corrupting their genetic code until the cells become dysfunctional and sometimes give up and die. These fierce radicals, built into life as both protectors and avengers, are the potent agents of aging."

It has been estimated that trillions of oxygen molecules go through our cells every day, inflicting hundreds of thousands of free radical hits or wounds on our cells' genes or DNA (based on research by geneticist Dr. Bruce Ames of the University of California at Berkeley). The body produces antioxidant enzymes that snip out and repair the genes, erasing about 99 percent of the damage to cells. But that still leaves thousands of wounded cells that go unrepaired. Over the years, these accumulate. By the time we reach middle age, there are perhaps a few million free radicals bouncing around and/or cellular rubbish produced by these radicals floating around in the body. These terrorists, along with the rusty junk of cellular protein produced by free radicals, push up the odds for infection and disease.

Dr. Earl R. Stadtman, researcher on aging with the National Institute of Health, has said, "Aging is a disease. The human life-span simply reflects the level of free radical oxidative damage that accumulates in cells. When enough damage accumulates, cells can't survive properly anymore and they just give up." The key to off-setting the aging process by slowing up the progress of disease is to aid the body in its fight with free radicals by taking supplements of antioxidants.

Solutions to Aging and Disease

Because of their molecular structure, antioxidants can give up electrons to replace the lost ones in the free radical atom, while not becoming harmful to other molecules in the process. So it is a good idea to flood the body with powerful antioxidants such as vitamin E, beta carotene, and vitamin C as well as garlic and PCO (Procyanidolic Oligomers found in grape seed extract).

The daily diet of an average person does not include enough vitamins, minerals, amino acids, and minerals to give the body everything it needs to fight free radicals and protect itself from disease. Plus, the food we eat today is of poorer quality because of the worn-out soil and over refined foods. The only way to get the right amount of nutrients is to take supplements. Special attention should be given to ensure all the vitamins, minerals, and trace elements are included in the supplements. But special attention should be given to potent antioxidants such as vitamins A, C, E, B1, B5, and B6, niacin, PABA, the trace elements zinc and selenium, and the amino acid cysteine.

One of the most important parts of a healthy immune system is the T-cell performance. T-cells eat up cancer cells and bacteria. They also consume fatty, hardened plaques which form in the walls of atherosclerotic arteries. Free radicals can destroy T-cells allowing plaque to build up and causing hardening of the arteries. A hefty dose of vitamin E (about 200 to 2,000 IU daily) can protect the T-cells and build up a resistance to heart disease and other diseases of aging.

Another important area of concern is the aging process of the brain's cells. As the body ages, it becomes more difficult to get oxygenated blood through rigid, narrowed capillaries of the brain. So as one ages senility sets in, which is accompanied by diminished concentration and short-term memory, increased absentmindedness, confusion, lack of energy, tiredness, depression, anxiety, dizziness, and tinnitus (ringing in the ears). One marvelous supplement to off-set this process is called ginkgo biloba (EGb). The ginkgo biloba tree is a 200-million-year-old tree that has survived just about everything you can imagine:

parasites, browsing animals, climate changes, molds, pollution, and disease. It has been called "a living fossil." A German botanist, Engelbert Kaempfer, discovered the ginkgo tree in 1690. The most amazing thing about the ginkgo leaves is they contain substances that seem to reverse the aging process. These substances, ginkgoheterosides and proanthocyanidines, make up about 47 per cent of ginkgo extract and have proven to be free radical quenchers, halting lipid peroxidation and protecting cell membranes.

In addition, ginkgo apparently assists blood to squeeze through the smallest vessels to nourish the brain, heart, and limbs. Tests have shown that patients memory has improved when they began taking ginkgo. More than 300 papers have been published on the power of ginkgo to stimulate blood flow feeding oxygen to tissues and the brain.

Another powerful antioxidant is Procyanidolic Oligomers (PCO), which was recently discovered to be at least 20 times more potent than vitamin C and 50 times more potent than vitamin E as an antioxidant. It is also anti-inflammatory, antiallergic, and antimutagenic. It is probably the most amazing nutrient discovered in the past 50-75 years. PCO is a bioflavonoid which the body needs, but cannot produce on its own. The best source for PCO is grape seed extract. PCO is named for its deep reddish purple color, which can be seen in the skins of grapes, cherries, blueberries, and other fruits. It is also found in the barks of lemon trees, Landis pine trees, and the leaves of hazelnut trees. PCO is more concentrated in grape seeds than any source.

If you want some powerful fighting forces to protect against disease and aging caused by free radicals, here are my suggestions for daily intake: 400 IU of vitamin E; 150-200 mg of grape seed extract; 60-120 mg of ginkgo biloba extract. In addition, I would also recommend a supplement of garlic.

Garlic has a strange mixture of chemicals which work as antibiotics, antiviral agents, cholesterol reducers, anticoagulants, blood pressure reducers, cancer inhibitors, decongestants, anti-inflammatory agents, and maybe even protectors of aging brain cells. When laboratory animals are fed garlic, they function better and live longer. The history of garlic goes back to the Chinese, where it is mentioned in the calendar of Hsai, in 2000 B.C. But a thousand years earlier, the Babylonians mentioned its use in inscriptions on the Great Pyramid at Gizeh in Egypt, where it is stated that the workers who built the Great Pyramid ate garlic.

Today there is a great deal of research supporting the positive effects of garlic on the body. For example, a study from Memorial Sloan Kettering Cancer Center in New York finds that garlic compounds actually stifle the growth of cancer cells. A Japanese study revealed that eating garlic can restore brain functioning and immune functioning in aged rats. Dr. Hiroshi Saito, professor of pharmaceutical sciences at the University of Tokyo, believes garlic may help prevent or even reverse Alzheimer's-like senility. Dr. Saito also found that garlic seems to stretch the lifespan of laboratory mice. Dr. Yongxiang Zhan, University of Tokyo, said, "Garlic's ability to impede the degeneration of the brain and immune system in aged animals is striking and impressive. That doesn't mean garlic can restore youth or completely block the aging process, but it can slow it down."

The best form to take garlic is fresh, either raw or cooked. The allicin, which gives garlic its odor, will strengthen two powerful antioxidant enzymes, catalase and gluthathione peroxidase, which are life extenders in lower forms of life. The next best way to take garlic is in capsule form. In one study, heart attack victims who ate a couple of cloves of garlic a day, raw or cooked, cut their odds of dying during the next two years by 66 percent! In supplement form, 400-800 milligrams daily will also prove to be beneficial.

In addition to grape seed extract, vitamin E, ginkgo biloba, and garlic, I would also recommend a daily dose of chromium. Chromium is an essential micronutrient, the central component of the glucose tolerance factor (GTF), which is essential in carbohydrate metabolism because it enhances the function of insulin. Chromium only binds with insulin if it is in the form of GTF. If the body is healthy, it produces its own GTF from chromium, niacin (vitamin B3), and certain amino acids. The problem is, about 90 percent of Americans have a chromium deficit. The reason this is such a problem is a person would have to eat 3,000 to 4,000 calories a day to get about 50 micrograms of chromium. When there is a low level of chromium, there will be an increased level of insulin which pollutes the bloodstream with high levels of blood sugar, bad LDL cholesterol, and triglycerides. Many people have insulin disorder, but do not realize it until irreparable damage is done. Chromium helps keep a normal balance of blood sugar and insulin.

A daily supplement of 100 to 300 micrograms of chromium will help in the following ways: lower insulin levels, lower triglycerides, raise the good HDL cholesterol, discourage artery clogging and heart disease, lower the bad LDL cholesterol, normalize blood sugar, thwart cancer, boost immune functioning, increase energy, increase lean body mass, and extend life.

The above supplements along with a good multivitamin taken daily will help strengthen the body's resistance to disease and aging.

There is also another important element to good nutrition: water. You should drink about 64 ounces of water spread throughout the day, which is about 8 glasses. A 32-ounce bottle filled twice a day will provide all the water the body needs. Consider some of the benefits:

1. Lose weight. Hunger is often thirst in disguise. Water will not only curb your appetite, but will help you to lose weight. Dr. Ellington Darden, former director of research for Nautilus Sports/Medical Industries and author of *32 Days to a 32-Inch Waist*, says that eight pints of ice water a day for four weeks will result in a loss of one pound. The body will expend 123 calories of body heat every day to warm that much ice water to a temperature of 98.6.
2. Be a sharper thinker. Dehydration caused by sweating can affect one's decision-making ability. A couple of glasses of water in hot weather can do wonders to sharpen your wits.
3. Relieve constipation. Plenty of fiber plus water equals good bowel movements which cleanse the intestines (preventing

leakage of waste through the intestinal walls), thus producing good health and increasing the energy level. I recommend a heaping tablespoon of psyllium husk in a glass of water.
4. Assist with jet-lag. The dry air on a plane can produce dehydration by sucking the water out of your system. That fatigued feeling you have during and after a flight may be from dehydration plus the lower level of oxygen in the plane. Drinking water before and during a flight can minimize the discomfort. It can be especially beneficial during international flights which can be 15-19 hours in length.

I have said very little about proper eating, which could fill a book by itself. Suffice to say, limit the amount of fatty foods and eat a balanced diet that includes plenty of vegetables with a sufficient amount of protein. I recommend staying away from red meat because of the fat and cholesterol it contains; however, a good red meat is ostrich, which is high in protein and lower in fat than beef and pork. A limited amount of white meat (fish and chicken) will be sufficient for your protein needs. Only a small amount of animal protein is necessary to meet protein requirements.

Stress

The third component of good health is reducing one's stress level. When a person experiences stress, the energy level is low and the mind is tired. Obviously, one way to combat stress is to follow the guidelines in this chapter on exercise and nutrition. I have discovered that a five-mile run can do more to reduce stress than almost anything else. The body has a chemical called beta-endorphin, which is released into the blood stream when the body is experiencing pain. These "natural opiates" are believed to produce what has been called "the runner's high," which many runners have experienced from time to time. Just 15 minutes of vigorous exercise can double the body's level of endorphin (norepinephrine). A study at Purdue University found that aerobic exercise improves problem-solving abilities and also enhances skills in forming strategies to solve complex problems. A study by psychologists at York University in Toronto concluded that marathon runners have significantly less anger, depression, and confusion than the average population. Dr. William Glassar believes that running puts one in touch with the right brain, which is the creative/problem solving side.

It is obvious from these studies that any kind of vigorous exercise will have beneficial results in lowering one's stress level, which will improve overall quality of life and possibly lengthen one's lifespan.

Another way to deal with stress is to take what I call "play breaks." Psychologist Dr. Rollo May, in *The Courage to Create*, discusses "the necessity of alternating work and relaxation, with the insight often coming at the moment of the break between the two, or at least within the break." Dr. May is right. If we can take a few moments away from what we are doing and allow the brain to think about something else, that little time away allows a diversion that can result in creative problem solving, which is a wonderful way to lower stress. Stress seems to come when there is not a balance between work and play. It is possible, therefore, to take "play breaks" during work.

Ann McGee-Cooper, in *You Don't Have to go Home From Work Exhausted*, suggests taking two- to five-minute breaks in order to develop a healthy balance of work and refreshing play or relaxation time during the work day. Here is a partial list she developed:

- Read the comics or your favorite columnist in the paper.
- Listen to a favorite song with a tape recorder and headphones.
- Close your eyes and visualize yourself skiing down a slope.
- Plan something enjoyable for that evening or weekend.
- Lay your head on the desk for a five-minute nap.
- Check the movie schedule in the daily paper.
- Call a friend and plan a lunch date.
- Praise a secretary or co-worker for a job well done.

- Browse through a catalogue or art book.
- Look at travel brochures and plan your next vacation.
- Play with a toy you keep at the office, such as a yo-yo, kaleidoscope, paddle ball, or dart board.
- Take a walk around the block or around the office.
- Work on a crossword puzzle.
- Breathe deeply or meditate for five minutes.
- Wash your face.
- Tell someone a joke.

The idea behind these "play breaks" is to give your brain an opportunity to focus on something different. Stress often comes because the brain has not been given an opportunity to think about ideas or projects that are not time sensitive. Ann McGee Cooper also suggests we should take five-minute, thirty-minute, even two-hour breaks away from demanding activities. These minivacations can refresh and relax. If the above list does not fit your personality, then make a list of your own. Try to think of at least 25 things you can do to take "play breaks" during your day.

The word that describes the above activity is "synergy." Synergy is combining what appear to be opposites within our lives and work. Psychologist Al Siebert has studied survivors of many different kinds of crises and has discovered that one of their most prominent characteristics is the ability to meld many opposites. Dr. Siebert states that the people who do well in crisis situations are those who can be both: serious and playful, tough and gentle, logical and intuitive, hard-working and lazy, shy and aggressive, introspective and outgoing, encouraging and demanding, supportive and confrontational, and so on. The word that would describe this type of person is *flexible*. They are people who can react to many different situations with responses that fit the need of the moment. Therefore, they do not feel like victims of the moment. They have the necessary skill and approach to handle whatever comes their way. The next chapter will give the keys to producing this kind of stress-free living.

Chapter 10

How to Communicate with Strong Emotion

In my final chapter on communications, I want to deal with two areas of communication which are often overlooked: the emotional and the spiritual. One may wonder how these areas contribute in any way to communication. But just as good health and nutrition make it possible to center in on others rather than being focused on self, even so, when one is in good emotional and spiritual health, there is an outward focus to life. This outward focus helps one to think about the needs of others and desire to communicate in order to understand and appreciate those needs. Again, the issue comes around to self-esteem. A person whose emotional and spiritual life is strong and confident is in a much better position to listen to and care about the needs, wants, and concerns of others.

The key to good emotional health is summed up in one word: responsibility. Once I take responsibility for the way I think and react, I am then empowered to take charge of my life. The flip side of that coin is to realize I am not responsible for the way others think and react. These two areas of thinking can free me from the victim mentality (blaming others for how I feel), and the controller mentality (trying to direct the lives of others).

Most of the emotional pain and suffering we experience is caused by self-blame and self-pity. These self-inflicting emotions usually result in anger and depression. They also block whatever happiness we might enjoy in life.

Bill Borcherdt, in *You Can Control Your Feelings!,* suggests the following self-accepting coping ideas:

- "Others' opinions don't equal who I am."
- "Approval is nice but not necessary."

- "I can stand and possibly even develop a high level of immunity to criticism."
- "I accept the challenge of not passing judgment on myself."
- "Often people won't pleasantly treat me in direct proportion to how nicely I treat them—tough beans!"
- "I'd best accept that fairness never has and probably never will exist."
- "I don't have to be the one person in the universe who always gets a fair return on emotional investment."
- "Others have a right to their opinion, but it does not represent me."
- "What I think of myself is much more important than what someone else thinks of me."
- "To be criticized is disappointing but not a disaster, sad but not tragic, a hassle but not a horror."

Dr. Viktor Frankl, who was a prisoner of the Nazis for four years, observed that the one freedom which could never be taken away is the freedom to choose one's attitude. "No one can harm me without my permission. They can harm my body, but they cannot harm me. I have control of that," Dr. Frankl declared. Dr. Frankl noted that the prisoners who chose to maintain hope were the ones who survived almost incredible human suffering, and the ones who chose to give up hope, died. What Dr. Frankl discovered is a truth that most have never discovered: There is no freedom without responsibility. When I take responsibility for my thoughts, I have found the greatest freedom available. No matter what my circumstances may be, I still have the choice of how I will view the situation and what I will think about it. No one can take that away or control it, unless I give my permission for that to happen.

Many of our moods or feelings are determined by how well we perform. We human beings tend to put ourselves on a performance rating, and then we decide how worthy we are based on how well we sang the song, ran the race, fixed the car, or sold the account. While this can be a very satisfying thing to do if the performance meets our standards, it has a hidden potential that can result in a devastating outcome if the performance is not up to par. A better way is to take on ideas that allow you to be successful or to fail and still accept yourself as a worthy person. When your emotional well-being is tied to your performance, your emotions are then subject to your ability, and not your value as a person, where they should be anchored.

Once you recognize the power of controlling and being responsible for your thought processes, you will discover the following advantages:

1. You can be yourself without fear. Most people feel they are on stage and their approval by others will determine how they feel about themselves. This can create a "false front," which is not the true person. But when you accept yourself, warts and all, you do not have to worry about what others think. You can relax and enjoy the person you are, and you will discover that others will enjoy you more as well.

2. You can become more courageous and experimental with life. When self-worth and emotional well-being are tied to performance, and success is found in some area, there is very little effort to venture out into strange or different areas because of a fear of failure. But if you understand you don't risk your value as a person by trying new things, there will be a willingness to become more adventuresome with life. If success is not achieved in the thing undertaken, at least something valuable has been learned from the experience. In any case, the emotional life is kept in balance. Life becomes an adventure rather than a rut that contains the same routine things day after day.

3. Your understanding and acceptance of others continues to grow. The attitude you take toward yourself is simply reflected in the attitude you take toward others. If you do not judge yourself on a performance basis, then you will not put others on the same level. Your acceptance of others will be based on their value as a human being and not on how well they measure up to your expectations.

4. You will be in better control of your emotions and thought processes. If you refuse to rate others based on performance, you will be a better listener and will discover things about others you would never know otherwise. In addition, you will be able to control your anger toward others when they do not perform as you expected, just as you control your anger toward yourself because you do not judge or condemn yourself when you fail to perform as expected. This type of open-mindedness toward yourself and others will result in a less stressful lifestyle and a more enjoyable way of relating to others. As a result of not requiring others to measure up or meet your standards, there will not be the flip-flopping of emotions which often occurs when others fail to perform; rather, there will be a more open and accepting attitude that can result in more clear-headed thinking.

5. You will become less ego-centered. When I was in high school, if one of the "popular" people refused to talk to me or indicated he/she did not want me around, I found it to be absolutely devastating emotionally. My whole self-esteem was tied to how well I was accepted by those who were supposed to be the "authorities" on who was accepted or rejected. So I spent my high school years in an ego-centered state, precisely where many others lived as well. What a great freedom it is to discover that others' opinion of me does not equal who I am. That one fact alone takes away so much pressure in interpersonal relationships. By refusing to be ego-centered, your conversation will be much more interesting because it will be open and focused on others. It is wonderful to be able to go through life without trying to please everyone around you, which, of course, is impossible anyway and ultimately leads to a letdown, because if you fail to measure up to others' expectations, some will reject you immediately. Eleanore Roosevelt said, "Nobody can make you feel inferior unless you give them permission."

6. Your esteem does not come from your achievement. It is nice to have successful accomplishments in life, but it is not necessary to have successful accomplishments in order to prove you are a worthy person. Making successful accomplishments demonstrates several positive characteristics such as skill, determination, creativity, and self-discipline. But these do not make you a valuable person; they simply add enjoyment to your appreciation of who you are as a person of worth. When you fail in an attempt to accomplish some project, that failure does not diminish you as a person; however, it does give you a chance to learn and grow from your failure. The freedom this way of thinking provides for you means you can enjoy the process because your esteem does not rest on the outcome!

7. You will stop the "check-list mentality." Success is a goal most people strive for in some way. I have a book lying on my desk at the time of this writing entitled *The Success Factor*. It is a very interesting and informative book on how to achieve success in one's career. The bottom line of the book is that success is achieved by reaching the goals one has set for himself/herself. Certainly setting and reaching goals is a wonderful thing to do. But if you are not careful, there is the possibility of developing an accountant mentality of keeping a ledger of accomplishments and/or goals and then placing value on yourself based on the check marks of success in the ledger. The greatest success in life, however, is to realize you can be successful without reaching the goals you've set. Part of the success is simply enjoying the journey and valuing yourself as a worthy person as you strive for the goals you've set. If, for some reason, you fail to reach the goal/s, you can still choose to feel positive about yourself, knowing that your value is not tied to the number of successful check marks on your "goals' ledger." This way of thinking frees you from blame and guilt, which are self-defeating ways of thinking that actually prevent you from reaching the goals you would like to accomplish in life.

8. You are no longer self-defensive. Most people go through life trying to protect themselves from the hurt and offense of others. One way to do that is to defend yourself when others accuse or blame you for some perceived or real failure in your life. Ultimately, that defensive reaction will fail, and you will either depreciate the other person or yourself, or maybe both. The results will be heard in statements such as: "You hurt me when you said...." "You make me so angry when you...." These statements come from a person who has not assumed responsibility for his/her emotional life. The individual is emotionally subject to the actions and/or reactions of others. Usually, the outcome of this is frustration and anger. We often become angry with those we depend on the most. The more emotionally dependent you are on another human being, the more anger you will have when that person lets you down. But if you have taken charge of your own life and emotional survival, then you know you are not dependent on another person for how you feel about yourself; consequently, your anger and depression are under the control of your thought processes rather than being subject to the treatment you receive from others.

9. You become a more ethical and moral person. Our ethics and morals are based on our value system. If you have a high value of yourself and, consequently, of others, your ethics/morals will be high as well. Morality grows out of the respect we have for others, and the respect we have for others grows out of the respect and value we place on ourselves. If you judge, condemn, and punish yourself for failures, you will tend to project the same behavior upon others. Obviously, there is unacceptable behavior which we see in the lives of others, but since I am not the judge and jury, I have no real right to sit in condemnation of another human being, no matter how reprehensible the person's behavior may be. Bill Borcherdt, in *Think Straight! Feel Great!*, observes: "The idea that people are the same as their behavior sets the guilt cycle in motion. People do their behavior, but they are not their behavior. To think

otherwise leads to self-blame when you do the wrong thing and other-blame when your companion is in violation." You have probably heard: *Love the sinner; hate the sin!* That old religious saw is exactly right! If you cannot separate the sin from the sinner in another person's life, you are likely unable to do the same in your life; therefore, you will judge and condemn yourself with every failure, rather than learning and growing from your mistakes. Judging and condemning will only lead to a reinforcement of the same behavior, because this kind of thinking tends to reinforce itself in actions.

Here is how it can work in just one example. If you are from an abusive home, it would be easy to judge and condemn your parents for their abuse of you. You then become angry toward them for their behavior. Consequently, you could also blame yourself for being a victim of abuse. Victims tend to find reasons to justify their victim mentality. In the above example, you might feel you could have prevented the abuse in some way, or, as a result of the abuse, you may feel inadequate as a person. So now you harbor anger toward your parents, and, indirectly, toward yourself. But if you are able to separate the "sin from the sinner," then you can rationally see that your parents did what they did because of reasons you may never fully understand. They, too, were victims in their own minds. The only way they knew how to deal with their victim mentality was to abuse you. But that abuse did not, in any way, reflect on your value as a person. You do not have to go through life angry, depressed, blaming yourself, or hating your parents. Just to have the permission to be free from those negative, self-defeating attitudes can be the most refreshing feeling in the world! The person you are today, or the person you want to be tomorrow, does not depend on what has happened to you in the past. Your failures can be stepping-stones to a better way of living. Your bad experiences can be growing and learning opportunities to help you love and appreciate others and be more tolerant of their behavior. The worn cliché *"This is the first day of the rest of your life"* has a lot of truth in it when you take responsibility for the way you think about yourself and the world in which you live.

When you realize you are not responsible for the behavior of others, but you are responsible for the way you think about yourself and others, then you are well on your way to good emotional health. Once you are free from the acceptance or approval of others, the basis for anger, anxiety, guilt, depression, stress, and frustration are removed. You no longer measure yourself or your self-worth on the assessment of others.

Happiness is a Choice

When reduced down to a common denominator, the goals all of us strive for in life are rooted in one major goal: happiness. The problem with happiness is we fail to understand where it is to be found. Richard A. Easterlin, an economist at the University of Southern California, in his new book *Growth Triumphant: The Twenty-First Century in Historical Perspective,* reports, "There has been no improvement in average happiness in the United States over almost a half century—a period in which real GDP per capital more than doubled." So having more money to buy more things does not, in itself, provide happiness. I realize that doesn't make sense to you when you have thought at one time or another, "If I just had a little more money to buy the things I want, I would be happier." In a sense, that is true. But with each step up the economic ladder, our desires seem to exceed our economic level. The average per person income in America since 1957 has grown from $9,000 (expressed in today's dollars) per year to over $18,000 per year today. This growth in income has given the average American incredible buying power. We eat out more and own more luxuries than at any other time in the history of this country. One would think our happiness ratio would be proportionately higher. But the opposite is true, we are actually less happy than we were four decades ago (based on research by the University of Chicago's National Opinion Research Center).

Traits of Happy People

In study after study, there are four basic traits that happy people possess:

1. *Self-Esteem.* I prefer to call it "self-value." Happy people are more likely to say, "I am a valuable person." "I am fun to be with." "I have good ideas." "I enjoy life." Notice these statements are positive thoughts expressed about self. Happy people believe they are intelligent, ethical, less prejudiced, able to get along with others, and opened minded. You can see that happy people have taken responsibility for their thoughts and have chosen to put value on themselves. They have chosen a positive outlook on life, not denying there are negative things in the world, but refusing to dwell on them. They do not look to others for their self-worth, but rather choose to believe the best about themselves.
2. *Personal Control.* Happy people have empowered themselves through their thought processes, and have, therefore, found success in almost every area of their lives. They tend to be better students, achieve more at work, and cope better with the stresses and strains of life. People who give up the control of their lives by giving up the control of their thoughts experience more depression, feel more like victims, and are often engaged in immoral activities (violation of the law, addictions, etc.). Consequently, people in low-income areas or people under totalitarian regimes or people in prisons, tend to be very unhappy because they feel controlled by others. But one does not have to be in those kinds of circumstances to feel controlled by others. Many people feel controlled by their mates, employers, and society in general. They develop the "victim mentality" that prevents them from choosing their own thoughts and determining their own destinies. Minorities in America often feel controlled by others, and, consequently, become victims of their own thinking processes. While it is true that some people are under the control and domination of others, the fact is, no one is under the mental control of another person, unless one chooses to be; therefore, a person could find happiness (if only momentarily) in almost any circumstance of life.

3. *Optimism.* Happy people have chosen to look at life optimistically. Poet Alexander Pope in a letter written in 1772, said, "Blessed is he who expects nothing, for he shall never be disappointed." That, of course, is one way to go through life without disappointment. But happy people go through life expecting good things. The outcome of this kind of thinking is what often is called: self-fulfilling prophecy. When you expect good things to happen, often they do. But when they don't, it is not the end of the world. There is always tomorrow, and there is always a new beginning... each day!

4. *Extroversion.* Jean-Paul Sartre once mused: "Hell is other people." One could conclude from that kind of thinking that the happiest people are those who stay to themselves and remain detached from the ups and downs of human relationships. But the opposite is true. The happiest people are those who enjoy being around others. However, there is a condition attached to this trait. Extroverts who are happy have chosen to relate to others without being emotionally dependent upon others. They can enjoy the company of others, and when they are alone, they can enjoy their *own* company. So we might say the happiest people are balanced extroverts/introverts. They can be alone without being lonely. They enjoy themselves! The happiest marriages are those in which both partners enjoy one another's companionship, but also realize each could live happily without the other. In this kind of relationship, there is no emotionally draining tug-of-war that pulls each other back and forth because of a perceived dependency on each other for emotional support. Infidelity in marriage often occurs when one partner looks outside the marriage for a relationship that does not drain him/her emotionally. The one thing that possibly could strengthen marriages more than any other is for both partners to become emotionally independent of each other.

The Spiritual Life

Sigmund Freud believed that religion is an illusion that erodes happiness and becomes a sort of sickness—an "obsessional neurosis" accompanied by guilt, repressed sexuality, and suppressed emotions. Freud was no doubt correct to a point. Many religions are powerful, mind-controlling, dominating institutions.

Yet, people who are religious seem to have a fuller, more satisfying, happier life. Why? Here are some possible reasons:

- The supportive relationships in the community of faith.
- The sense of meaning and purpose in life that religious faith provides.
- The motivation to focus beyond self.
- The belief there is something even better beyond the few years of this life.
- The belief that life, both now and hereafter, is directed by a loving, benevolent Creator.
- The hope that death does not end one's existence.

These are excellent reasons for believing in the spiritual part of life. But beyond these, there are some other reasons for believing there is more to this life than "meets the eye."

Basically, the spiritual life comes down to a simple question: Is there a Power/Force (a God) beyond the laws that operate within the context of this universe? Some believe there is no outside Power responsible for the universe, others believe there is a Power operating outside the universe, and some believe there is not enough evidence to believe one way or the other.

There is a story about an old Jewish rabbi who was talking to a learned philosopher. The philosopher said that even though he respected the rabbi, nevertheless, it was impossible for him to believe in God and that the universe, the world, and life all came into being through natural means, without outside intervention.

The rabbi said nothing in reply, but some time later returned to the philosopher with a profoundly moving poem written on parchment in the most glorious calligraphy.

The philosopher, seriously impressed, inquired as to the artist and poet. The rabbi told him there was no poet or artist. He explained that the paper was lying on his desk when a cat knocked over the inkwell.

The philosopher said, "That's simply impossible. Somebody must have written the poem and somebody obviously put it to paper!"

The rabbi replied, "You said yourself that the universe, the world and life, which are more beautiful and wondrous than any poem, came into being by themselves. Why do you doubt the same for this simple, humble poem?"

Simplistic thinking? Perhaps. But in another sense, it is profound in its implications. Things do come down to those two choices. Either we are products of some intelligent design, or we are products of chance happenings.

David Green and Robert Goldberger, in *Molecular Insights Into the Living Process* (New York: Academic Press, 1967), pp. 406-407, write: "However, the macromolecule-to-cell transition is a jump of fantastic dimensions, which lies beyond the range of testable hypothesis. In this area, all is conjecture. The available facts do not provide a basis for postulating that cells arose on this p l a n e t.... We simply wish to point out the fact that there is no scientific evidence." Hubert P. Yockey, in "A Calculation of the Probability of Spontaneous Biogenesis by Information Theory," *Journal of Theoretical Biology*, Vol. 67, p. 398, also observes: "One must conclude that, contrary to the established and current wisdom, a scenario describing the genesis of life on earth by chance and natural causes which can be accepted on the basis of fact and not faith has not yet been written."

The purpose in giving the above quotes is to establish the fact that whatever one chooses to believe about how we got here remains in the area of faith, not fact. With that having been established, the question is: Which faith option gives one the greatest assurance and hope?

Perhaps many arguments could be given on behalf of any one of the three approaches (theism, atheism, agnosticism). I would like to give the one argument that carries the most weight in my thinking.

The argument (I prefer the word evidence) is called *Irreducible Complexity*. The phrase was developed by Dr. Michael Behe, associate professor of biochemistry, department of biological sciences, Lehigh University. He illustrates it very simply in a paper presented in the Summer of 1994 at the meeting of the C.S. Lewis Society, Cambridge University:

> *Consider the humble mousetrap. The mousetraps that my family uses in our home to deal with unwelcome rodents consist of a number of parts. There are: (1) a flat wooden platform to act as a base; (2) a metal hammer, which does the actual job of crushing the little mouse; (3) a wire spring with extended ends to press against the platform and the hammer when the trap is charged; (4) a sensitive catch which releases when slight pressure is applied; and (5) a metal bar which holds the hammer back when the trap is charged and connects the catch. There are also assorted staples and screws to hold the system together.*
>
> *If any one of the components of the mousetrap (the base, hammer, spring, catch, or holding bar) is removed, then the trap does not function. In other words, the simple little mousetrap has no ability to trap a mouse until several separate parts are all assembled.*
>
> *Because the mousetrap is necessarily composed of several parts, it is irreducibly complex. Thus, irreducibly complex systems exist.*
>
> *Now, are any biochemical systems irreducibly complex? Yes, it turns out that many are.*

Dr. Behe goes on to list things like proteins, including aspects of protein transport, blood clotting, closed circular DNA, electron transport, the bacterial flagellum, telomeres, photosythesis, transcription regulation, and much more. Dr. Behe states that examples of irreducible complexity can be found on virtually every page of a biochemistry textbook.

It seems to me this is one of the most powerful arguments in favor of a Creator-God. Most arguments in favor of a Supreme Creator center in the stars, planets, and conformity of living things to adapt to one another and live in a world with all the basic requirements for continuation of life. These, of course, are strong arguments. But the astonishing array of chemical machines, made up of finely calibrated, interdependent parts that defy current naturalistic explanations, seem to point to a superb intelligence that designed them to work together in complexity.

Dr. Behe states that he has no quarrel with the idea of common descent. Neither do I. Nor do I have a quarrel over the issue of how long it took for life as we know it to arrive at this point. It may well have been billions and billions of years, as the late Dr. Carl Sagan would put it. Intelligent design of life may mean the ultimate explanation of life is beyond scientific exploration and discovery. The point, in my way of thinking, is not how long (or even how) a Creator-God would or could take to develop life, but the real issues involve these questions: Are we products of chance or of creation? Which one gives the greater value to each human being? Which one gives me the ability to look at my life with value and high esteem? Which one puts me on the same level with all other human beings (without viewing some races as lower forms of human beings on the evolutionary ladder)?

The answer to all these questions for me is belief in a Creator-God, who lovingly placed all human beings on this planet for reasons we may never fully comprehend in this life. He/She obviously has provided for us opportunities for growing, learning, experimenting, and exploring. Through our struggles, pains, sufferings, and trials, we learn valuable lessons about discipline, love, tolerance, and grace. These valuable qualities make us more respectful and better able to sympathize and empathize with one another. As we learn more about who we are in relationship to our world and to one another, we continue to evolve into stronger, more intelligent people. We learn how to deal with our problems by helping, caring, and sharing. As a result of all this, the world becomes a better place in which to live. We learn how to communicate with tolerance and understanding. We discover that wars are not the answers to our disagreements; neither is prejudice, nor racism, nor bigotry. We begin to see all religions and faiths as human beings struggling to better understand their world and themselves.

And isn't that the basis for good communication for the 21st century?

Appendix

How to Communicate as an Emphatic Listener

As an addendum to all the areas of communications I have covered in this book, it is important to underscore the power of listening. Even though I have touched on the subject in some of the chapters, I want to give some specific thoughts about it here.

Dean Rusk once said, "The best way to persuade people is with your ears—by listening to them." Diane Sawyer said, "I think the one lesson I have learned is that there is no substitute for paying attention." Rene McPherson said, "The way to stay fresh is you never stop traveling, you never stop listening. You never stop asking people what they think." Sam Walton said, "The key to success is to get out into the store and listen to what the associates have to say. It's terribly important for everyone to get involved. Our best ideas come from clerks and stockboys." Oliver Wendell Holmes wrote, "It is the province of knowledge to speak. And it is the privilege of wisdom to listen." Karl Menninger said, "Listening is a magnetic and strange thing, a creative force. The friends who listen to us are the ones we move toward. When we are listened to, it creates us, makes us unfold and expand."

Perhaps the greatest compliment paid to Princess Diana after her tragic death was this one which appeared in the editorial of *Christian Science Monitor*, September 2, 1997: "Like the Barb's King Harry before Agincourt she (Princess Diana) captured the hearts of the footsoldiers of a nation, wandering among her fellow Britons and listening."

Ralph Nicols said, "The most basic of all human needs is the need to understand and be understood." Stephen Covey, in his audio tape series *7 Habits of Highly Effective People*, states: "The habit of communication is one of the master skills in life, the key to building win-win relationships, and the essence of professionalism. We see the world as we are, not as it is. Our perceptions come out of our experiences. As people from both sides interact, they sometimes question the credibility of those who see it differently. To resolve these difficulties and to restore credibility, one must exercise empathy, seeking first to understand the point of view of the other person."

All of these quotes emphasize the importance of good listening, a skill no one learns in school. It has to be developed. When we think about communication, most of us think about talking . . . having a good command of the language, smooth delivery, proper grammar, etc.

If you wanted to improve your communications skills, the local university or community college probably has several courses you could take in speech and communication. But I would venture to say there will not be one course on how to become a good listener. Yet, there can be no real communication without this taking place, hopefully, in two-way communication.

To help you develop the skills of an emphatic listener, here are some suggestions that will help you become a better listener:

1. *Maintain eye contact.* Force yourself to look at the other person (not stare), while he/she is talking. This helps you to stay focused and encourages the other person to be more open and honest. Eye contact says: I care about you and want to hear what you have to say.

2. *Pay close attention.* Do you find yourself partially listening to the other person while, at the same time, composing your response to what is being said? The problem is you assume you know what is going to be said before it is said. The reason this often happens is the brain hears a key word and begins to form an idea from that word. Here is a little game that illustrates how it works:

How many of each animal did Moses put on the Ark?

Most would answer two because "animal" and "Ark" become key words. But the answer, of course, is none because Moses did not put animals on the Ark, Noah did.

Here is another example:

Spell pop. Spell top. Spell mop. What are you supposed to do at a green light? When you ask those questions verbally, almost everyone will say, "Stop." The words pop, top, mop would lead the mind to say stop. Here is another one.

Spell host. Spell most. What do you put in a toaster? Almost everyone will say toast. But you don't put toast into a toaster.

3. *Use the power of the question.* Paraphrasing a statement back to the speaker in the form of a question is a wonderful way to be sure you understand what was said. Here is an example of how it works: "Are you having a hard time deciding what to do about your job because you fear making the wrong decision?" Instead of thinking about what you want to say in response to the comments of another person, ask more questions and you may discover a deeper level of understanding.

4. *Watch your body language.* Closing off your body by folding your arms across the chest, or fidgeting, or looking around all communicate inattention to the speaker. But they also cause you to lose concentration. Keeping open posture, leaning toward the speaker with good eye contact will help you to stay focused on what the person is saying.

5. *Make notes.* There are some situations in which notetaking is an appropriate thing to do, even in conversation. Make it a habit to write things down. This is one of the best listening tools you can possess. After the conversation, review what you wrote. This helps you to double check your understanding and impression of the conversation. By the way, this also communicates a caring attitude toward the person speaking.

6. *Ask the person to repeat a statement.* If you are not clear about what was said, don't hesitate to ask the person to repeat what was said. This can especially be a problem if you don't hear well.

7. *Watch the facial expressions.* As you listen to another person, look at the facial expressions. What do you see? We

human beings express many different emotions through our facial expressions: sadness, happiness, confusion, love, fear, anger. By watching the facial expressions of the speaker, you will be able to go past the words to find the emotions being felt at that moment. Then you will hear not only what is being said, but what the person is trying to say as well. You will sense the whole truth about the message instead of receiving it piecemeal.

8. *Use the pause.* When the speaker stops talking, wait a few moments before responding. Some have suggested counting to 5 before speaking. That is probably a good idea; in any case, give the person plenty of time to finish the thought. Look at the body language and watch the facial expressions. You can often tell if he/she is thinking about what to say next or has finished. Usually, if the person has finished, he/she will look at you with a "what do you think" expression. That can be your cue to either ask a question or paraphrase what you've heard or both.

One of the ways you communicate a caring attitude is to actively listen to the other person. In some of the research on listening between couples, the longest period of attentive listening was 17 seconds. It is no surprise most marriages have real communication problems!

But in every area of human relationships, the lack of emphatic listening seems to be a problem. I felt it was important to close out this book by giving some guidelines on this important aspect of good communications. As we become more and more advanced in the use of sophisticated equipment for communications, nothing will ever replace one human being talking to another human being, heart to heart, about life.

For a final thought, here is a quote from *Pooh's Little Instruction Book*, inspired by A. A. Milne:

> "If the person you are talking to doesn't appear to be listening, be patient. It may simply be that he has a small piece of fluff in his ear."

Bibliography

Adler, Alfred. *What Life Could Mean to You*. Chatham, New York: One World Publication, 1992.

Axtell, Roger E. *Do's and Taboos Around the World*. White Plains, New York: Benjamin Books, 1985.

Behe, Michael. *Darwin's Black Box—The Biochemical Challenge to Evolution*. New York: Free Press, 1996.

Borcherdt, Bill. *Think Straight! Feel Great!* Sarasota, Florida: Professional Resource Exchange, Inc., 1989.

Carper, Jean. *Stop Aging Now!* New York: HarperCollins, 1995.

Cooper, Ann McGee. *You Don't Have to go Home From Work Exhausted*. New York: Bantam Books, 1990.

Giblin, Les. *How to have Confidence and Power in Dealing with People*. Englewood Cliffs, N. J.: Prentice—Hall, Inc., 1956

Glass, Lillian. *Talk to Win*. New York: Perigee Books, 1987.

Glover, Bob & Shepherd, Jack. *The Runner's Handbook*. New York: Viking Peguin, Inc., 1977.

Goleman, Daniel. *Emotional Intelligence*. New York: Bantam Books, 1995.

Hess, E. *The Tell-Tale Eye*. New York: Van Nostrand Reinhold, 1975.

Hoff, Ron. *I Can See You Naked*. Kansas City: Andrews and McMeel,1992.

James, Jennifer. *Thinking in the Future Tense*. New York: Simon & Schuster, 1996.

Jandt, Fred. *The Customer is Usually Wrong!*. Indianapolis, IN: Park Ave Publications, 1995.

Pease, Alan. *Signals: How to use Body Language for Power, Success and Love*. New York: Bantam Books, 1981.

Peters, Tom.*Thriving on Chaos*. New York: Random House, 1987.

Peters, Tom & Austin, Nancy. *A Passion for Excellence.* New York: Random House, 1985.

Price, Jonathan. *Put That in Writing.* New York: Penguin Books, 1984.

Rogoff, Leonard and Ballenger, Grady. *Office Guide to Business Letters, Memos & Reports.* New York: Macmillan, 1994.

Rosenbaum, Dr. Michael E. *The Chromium Connection.* Novato, CA: Nutrition Encounter, Inc., 1990.

Sabath, Ann Marie. *Business Etiquette in Brief.* Holbrook, Massachusetts: Bob Adams, Inc., Publishing, 1993.

Schaaf, Dick. *Keeping the Edge—Giving Customers the Service They Demand.* New York: Hudson Books, 1995.

Sharon, Dr. Michael. *Complete Nutrition.* Garden City Park, NY: Avery Publishing Group, Inc., 1994.

Stewart, Marjabelle Young and Faux, Marian. *Executive Etiquette in the New Workplace.* New York: St. Martin's Press, 1979.

Timm, Paul R. *50 Powerful Ideas You Can Use to Keep Your Customers.* Hawthorne, NJ: The Career Press, 1992.

Walters, Lilly. *Secrets of Successful Speakers.* New York: McGraw-Hill, Inc., 1993.

Whiteley, Richard C. *The Customer Driven Company.* Reading, Mass: Addison-Wesley Publishing Company, 1991.

Willingham, Ron. *Hey, I'm the Customer.* Englewood Cliffs, NJ: Prentice-Hall, 1992.

Index

ACSI (American Customer Satisfaction Index) 120
Active voice writing, 49-50
Adjectives, 63
Adverbs, 63
Aerobic exercise, 131
Aggressive persons, 39
Aging, 134
Air travel, 95
Alphabet (first), 45
American method of eating, 85
Anger and assertiveness, 42
Antecedents, 78
Antioxidant enzymes, 135
Apostrophe, 76
Assertive person, 31-33,39
Body language, 8
Brackets, 74
Brainstorming, 49
C's, 7 of writing, 59
Capitalization, 80
Check-list mentality, 147
Chromium, 138-139
Clichés, 55
Colon, 70
Comma, 68,69
Complaining customers, 117
Complex sentence, 66
Compound sentence, 66
Compound-complex sentence, 67
Conjunctions (correlative), 65
Conjunctions, 64
Continental method of eating, 85
Could of / should of, 80
Customer-centered culture, 124
Customer-loving people, 123
Customer-obsessed movement, 121
Dash, 74
Deep-body breathing, 9
Different than / from, 80
Dissatisfied customer, 116
Double comparisons, 79
Double negatives, 77
E-plus thinking, 113-114

Egotists, 104
Ellipsis, 72
Emotional intelligence, 99
Equality, 38
Exceptional Customer Service, 113
Exclamation mark, 76
Exercise, 129
Extroversion, 152
Eye contact, 160
Eye contact, 21
FACS (facial action coding system), 20
Fight or flight syndrome, 2
Fogging, 35-36,37
Folding the arms, 23
Frankl, Dr. Viktor, 144
Free radical oxidative damage, 135
Free radicals, 134
Garlic, 137-138
Gender-free writing, 56,57
Gift giving, 89
Ginkgo biloba, 136
Global leaders, 107
Global respect, 88
Global thinker, 107
Grape seed extract, 137
Greek factor, 5
Handshakes, 25-27
Happiest marriages, 152
Happiness, 150
Headlines, 58
Hyphen, 72
Impulse control, 102
Interjections, 65
Internet, the, 117
Intonation, 10
Introductions, 88
Irreducible complexity, 155-156
Jargon, 54
Job interviewing, 91-94
K.I.S.S., 13
Killer fillers, 10
Laliophobia, 2
Lifelong learning, 108
Like /as, 78

Index

May, Dr. Rollo, 141
Mehrabian, Dr. Albert, 19
Messages: "I," "you," 34-35
Method, the, 3
Mind-mapping, 49
Monotone, 10
Mood management, 100
Negative assertion, 38
Negative body language, 22
Negative inquiry, 37
Nervousness as power, 2
Nonverbal communication, 28,29
Open palms, 21
Open posture, 21
Optimism, 152
Oral resonance, 9
Ostrich, 140
Paragraphs (short), 57
Parenthesis, 73
Passive persons, 39
Passive voice writing, 49,50
People skills, 103
Period, 71
Personal control, 151
Play breaks, 141
Positive thinking, 41
Prepositions, 63
Pronouns, 62
Pulitzer, Joseph, 59
Question mark, 75
Quotation marks, 74
Rapid thinking, 14
Rate of speech, 10
Reader-centered writing, 46,48

Redundant writing, 53,54
Reframing anger, 101
Road rage, 96
Role models, 41
Rule of three, 6
Sagan, Dr. Carl, 156
Self-awareness, 100
Self-defensive, 148
Self-esteem, 32, 151
Self-motivation, 101
Self-Talk (positive), 39
Semicolon, 70
Service quality, 127
Simple sentence, 66
Speaking, joy of, 17
Spiritual life, 153
Stress, 140
Synergy, 142
T-cells, 136
Table manners, 84
Target zone, 131
Theater of the mind, 10
Top-down writing, 48
Total product concept, 115
Unparalleled sentences, 79
Verbs, 63
Victim mentality, 149
Visuals, 7-8
Voice of judgment, 3
Webser, Daniel, 1
Wordiness, 51
Working a room, 27
Workplace diversity, 90
World brain pool, 107
Ziglar, Zig, 14